Acknowledgements

I would like to thank my Family who loves and supports me in everything I do, y'all make it easy to be who I am.

I would also like to say thank you to My Husband who has given me so much over the years and continues to each day, Thank you James. Thank you to my daughters, Laila and Sasha. And thank you to my mother.

I would like to thank Mary and Jason who have helped me in so many ways and have allowed me to continue doing what I love each day as well as helping others on their journey's in life.

I would like to thank Camille Thomas, who has helped me organize and create many of my Level Up books and more. Thank you Camille, for making my dream of being an author possible with your talent and skills and all of your help thus far.

Leveling Up To Your Best Life

Creating A Life of Comfort and Luxury

Table of Contents

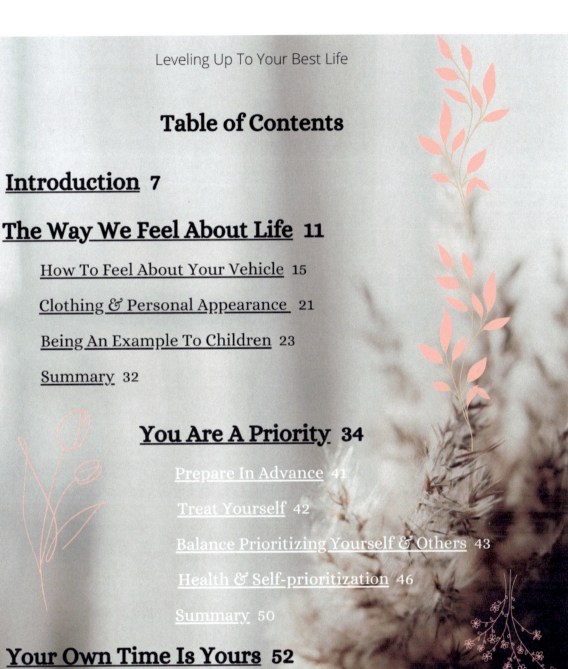

Table of Contents

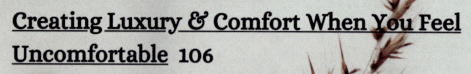

Table of Contents

Table of Contents

This book was created to teach you how to enjoy and make your life one that you actually want to live.

This book is needed more than ever at this time particularly due to the ways that people perceive life, including the use of technology and how it seems to affect perspective.

This book will show you that you already have the tools to live and relish in your own life and that they have been there the entire time.

Do you feel like each day of your life is a repeat of the day before? Do you feel like all you do is work or go to school and never get to enjoy the lifestyle of comfort and luxury? This book shows you how. No matter what type of budget you have, with less than a few dollars you can create the feeling of luxury and comfort for yourself.

For example, when you stumble in from a long day of work, school, or just a busy day of running errands, do you arrive home to even more work, tasks and a place that makes you feel as if you are not where you want to be in your own life? With less than $5 you can feel as if you are arriving home to a place of luxurious comfort and style.

How? You ask?

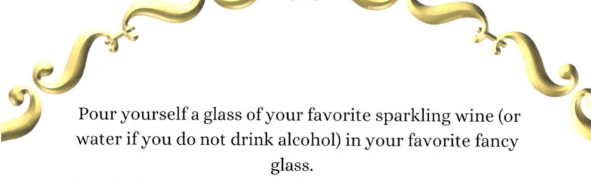

Pour yourself a glass of your favorite sparkling wine (or water if you do not drink alcohol) in your favorite fancy glass.

If you do not own a fancy glass, you can make one for a few dollars with some cement glue, an old earring or brooch and a wine glass. Suddenly, you have a glass you cannot wait to rush home to sip your choice of evening beverage from.

Next, add a candle of your chosen scent for soft ambiance lighting and aromatherapy. Turn on your favorite classical music or even a soundscape of nature sounds. I like to pair my phone to a wireless speaker and find an ambiance audio or video that lasts for hours.

Now you need your favorite snack that is always in stock in your pantry since it is your favorite. Take the snack out of the packaging and place it on a plate.

Slip into your most elegant robe or pajamas while you sit, taste your favorite bites on a plate and sip from a fancy glass, listening to the sounds of classical music or your ambient soundscape. If you were to be photographed in this moment, you would look as if you were living an exquisite life of comfort, style and luxury.

I have done this with my daily life and it has changed the mundane into a life I've always wanted and already had. I just never tried to make it as special as it could be.

This book is for those who want to create special moments in their daily lives and give more meaning and satisfaction to the routines we seem to have taken the magic and romance out of. We can have the life we seem to be searching for if we create the moments exactly how we want them.

Your life will tremendously benefit from living on purpose. Each day you wake up, you know that your own life is going to be one that brings pleasure, luxury, comfort and meaning to you and the others that are lucky enough to know you.

Your level up of the mundane in your life is where leveling up feels the best.

It is easy to buy a set of furniture, live in a nice house and drive a nice car, but how easy is it to feel satisfied and full of enjoyment when at home, sitting on the furniture or driving someplace? Leveling up the moments that you overlook is what actually levels up your lifestyle no matter how much money you have.

I have seen many people shop and buy expensive items, yet never seem to enjoy using them or receiving comfort from them. Some people buy what looks expensive in order to try and feel that they have a lifestyle of luxury and comfort they believe they should have. Yet, they still shop and never figure out how to enjoy their own lives with what they already have.

Meanwhile, there are thrifty men and women who live lavishly while spending less. Learn how this is done and so much more.

Love,

The Way We Feel About Life

Have you accepted your life as is? This is a question most people would not tend to ask themselves. Yet, they should. The way you feel about your life is what you have accepted and how you feel about that acceptance. Ask yourself, if you have accepted life as it is. If the answer is yes, ask yourself if you like the way you live your life. Chances are, you may feel that your own life could use some improvements. You may feel like your lifestyle could be more leveled up, yet you may not know where to start or you may feel you don't have the budget to live a leveled-up lifestyle. What if I told you that you could feel the comfort and luxury of a leveled-up lifestyle daily?

First, you need to feel as if you deserve the leveled-up lifestyle. Then, you need to feel as if you were destined to live a life of comfort and luxury. This is best done by writing in a journal about how you want to feel each day you wake up. Do not write about the material items of luxury that you want to acquire. Write about how such items will make you feel inside about yourself. Now ask yourself if those items will make you feel the same way every day in a year from now. Do you personally know someone who has the material items you want, and do you feel they are living a leveled up comfortable life?

The way you feel about your life is what you have accepted and how you feel about that acceptance...

How To Feel About Your Vehicle

Most of the material items we want can be purchased, but the feeling we get from those items are not usually long lasting. It's like when you get a new car, you are so excited to get up and drive it. You take photos of it, wash it and pick up each tiny speck of lint, or any litter you might see on the seats or floor.

Do you still feel the same way about your car now as you did the first week you purchased it? Chances are you still like your car, but you do not get that same feeling of euphoria that it once gave you. This is what needs to be replenished. This is the feeling that allows you to feel the comforts and luxuries of life. What would it take for you to feel the same way about your car now as you did when you bought it?

What is in your car? Do you keep a nice umbrella or a pair of special sunglasses in it?

Do you have a special place for your phone, keys, purse etc.? Do you have a signature scent for your car or a seasonal air freshener? Many of us have these.

- Did you make your signature scent?
- Is your umbrella in your favorite color/pattern, or plain?
- Do you have a keychain or something meaningful to you on your keyring?
- Do you have a classical or jazz playlist? Or a radio station set with other music you like to listen to?
- Are you well put together when you leave your home?
- Does your clothing and your car look nice together or clash?

I feel that all of these factors could play a role in how you feel about your car. I find that when I dress nice and look good, I feel good when getting into my car. My car matches my style which is well put together. I keep it maintained. If you try to always look your best when you go somewhere, you should be sure to keep your car decent as well. There is nothing like walking out of a restaurant or store and getting into a clean car, even if it is not your dream car. It sparkles and shines. It could even be someone else's dream car. We forget sometimes that what we have can be what others are striving for. So treat your vehicle like what someone who is striving for something similar would.

We forget sometimes that what we have is similar to what others are striving for...

The more you value what you already have, the more value you see in it. Try this. Think about someone who dreams of purchasing a car similar to the one you are currently driving. Now feel how excited they must feel when they see you drive by giving them a glimpse of what they are striving for.

Now how do you feel about your current car? That is the feeling of comfort and luxury as well as appreciation for what you already have. Imagine yourself well-dressed and getting into your car and that person who is aspiring towards the same suddenly views their own potential. With your well-put-together attire and clean car, you may give that person more to look forward to each day as they strive for what you have shown is possible for themselves.

If your style and car need work, work with what you have and can afford. Do not overspend.

If your car is not the car you like, then appreciate the function of the car and how it gets you to the places that you need to go. If your car is older or not in the best condition, keep it clean and well maintained. Now I know driving a car that may not seem desirable to others is not the best feeling, but having a running car that works is a great feeling as well. Think of a person who does not have a car, or a person who does not have a working vehicle. Try to feel how difficult it must be for them to get to the places they need to go. Now think about them looking at you in your well-put-together outfit getting into your car and driving away while they are walking or waiting on a ride.

How you should feel when you get into your car is like you feel now. This is the feeling of comfort and the luxury of your current vehicle.

Clothing & Personal Appearance

Simple monotone outfits such as matching slacks, skirts, sweaters, tops and jackets always look elegant if the style and fit is elegant as well. Looking elegant helps you to feel elegant. This feeling leads to acting elegant. Acting this way then leads to actually being elegant. Choose a pair of shoes that are appropriate for where you are going. If you will be walking a lot, opt for a pair of flats or loafers. If you won't be doing much walking, wear a pair of heels or dress shoes. Sneakers belong in the gym, the park and on kids in my opinion, but to each their own.

How do you feel in your effortless elegant outfit that you put together with the pieces you already have in your closet? Imagine going to the store in that same outfit and receiving compliments on your attire. Now think about someone else who is wearing a pair of pajamas and slippers in the store witnessing you receiving compliments. They may have the same basic pieces in their wardrobe to look as effortlessly elegant as you look. But now, you may have inspired that person want to level up their look and style. The feeling you get while receiving compliments on your effortless elegance is the feeling of a leveled up luxurious lifestyle. This is why I say, luxury, comfort and a leveled-up lifestyle is how you *feel* about your own life and how you *feel* about yourself.

Taking the basic parts of our lives and making

them extraordinary allows us to live life in a whole new way.

Being An Example To Children

Some of us have children, so we tend to try to save time by not putting much effort into our own appearance and daily routine. Some of us put more effort into making our children look more put together than ourselves. This is where many of us go wrong. By not putting effort into your own looks and selfcare, you are showing your children that it's not really important to you or important in adulthood to put effort into how you look or how you approach your daily routines. They probably won't see the value in all of your efforts to make them look and feel better than you (the parent). Children usually mimic who they look up to and admire.

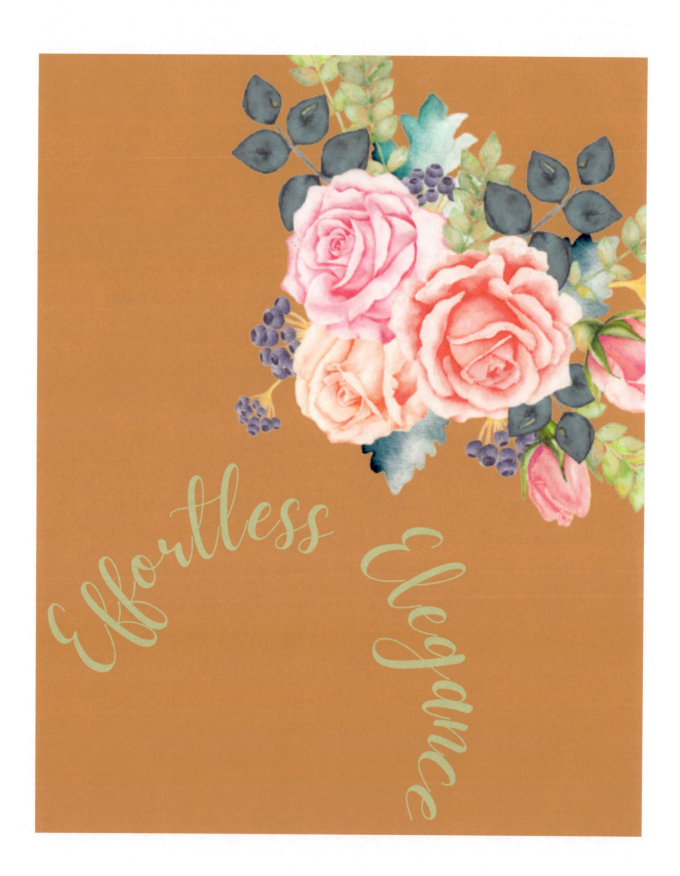

Effortless Elegance

If your children look at you and do not admire what they see or how you live each day, they may decide to look elsewhere and mimic someone who fits their ideal look and lifestyle, leaving you, the parent(s) with less influence over them.

If you want your children to have nice clothing, and appreciate the lifestyle that you give to them, then you need to also start wearing nicer attire, and live and appreciate your current lifestyle. We teach by example. If you wake up and put on an elegant robe and slippers, make your coffee or tea in a fancy cup and saucer set, and sit at your table to enjoy your morning beverage, your children will most likely see that as the norm. They will follow that same example with their own routines.

Make sure if you have a robe and slippers, that they also have a robe and slippers.

If you drink out of a fancy cup, make sure they have a fancy cup as well. When your example of the way you live life is not balanced with what you expect of your children, they may not understand the reason you expect them to do more than you are willing to do for yourself. This could also allow them to see you as less valuable since that is how you appear and seem to them by your example.

The opposite of this can be seen in some families as well. When you see the parents dressed up and looking their best and the children looking a mess. This may be due to a lack of time or a clash in what the children and parents deem as stylish. I know by experience how clothing styles can clash due to current trends and styles that may seem sloppy or not well put together as far as clothing is concerned.

Then there is the issue of hairstyles. In some cases, the children may want to show their independence by wanting to style their own hair. I know I was one of these children growing up. I did not like how my mother styled my hair so I took the task of styling it myself.

Needless to say, I was not the best looking 5th grader on picture day, but I was happy because I was not 11 years old wearing several ponytails with bows, clips and ribbons all over my head. That was not the style nor trend as a 5th grader about to go to middle school. I also was allowed to dress myself and pick out my own outfits because I had very different tastes in what was stylish than what my mother thought was fashionable.

I chose to be creative and made outfits that would allow me to express my own personal style.

Now this personal style was not what I would call, posh or elegant at the time, but it allowed me to live the life I felt I wanted to live. I did not feel controlled or obligated to wear what my parents thought I should wear. This is important in life; that you do not feel obligated or pressured to live in a certain way that is not comfortable nor your definition of luxurious. To a child comfort and luxury could be allowing them to choose their own style. My robe may be made of satin, while their robe has their favorite character or color. We don't have to have the same style to feel the same comfort and luxury as our children. We only need to have the tools to give to them so that they also can live their lives in full appreciation of what they have. When you don't grow up with this feeling, you may tend to search for it in other ways.

If you are a single parent and raising a child of the opposite sex, be sure to allow more masculine and or feminine options for them to choose from so that they are not only getting the benefits of one gender. Be sure to complement and admire others who you deem as handsome or pretty in the child's presence so they too know how you perceive a man and a woman's efforts in their appearance too. It is important to show children that you value and appreciate others who also make efforts to look and live life with leveled-up standards.

This is important in life; that you do not feel obligated or pressured to live in a certain way that is not comfortable nor your definition of luxurious...

Watch movies with appropriate role models of the opposite sex and be sure to comment on how you approve of the character's role and their actions in the film. Children will focus and give more attention to these sort of role models when watching films and perhaps adopt some of their morals and standards that they may not get from you as a member of the opposite sex.

Don't feel guilty or as if you are not providing your child with what they need if you are a single parent. Instead, focus on showing your child what you need to show them, so they are provided with the proper examples of what is favorable and leveled up by your standards. Also, allow your children to tell you who they admire and why, so that you have an idea of who they deem to be good role models. This gives you the chance as a parent to see if the child knows what a good example of the opposite sex is, then you can compromise from there.

Summary

- Live your life as if you actually appreciate all that you already have.
- Make the most out of what you already have.
- Be an example of living your life by your standard of feeling leveled up
- Know that luxury and comfort are feelings, not material items.
- Put effort into your daily routines to take them from basic to enjoyable and meaningful.
- Teach your children to live their lives the same way by example.

In the next chapter, you will learn...

To allow yourself to feel like a priority. If you feel like you are a priority to yourself, others will also treat you as though you are a priority to them.

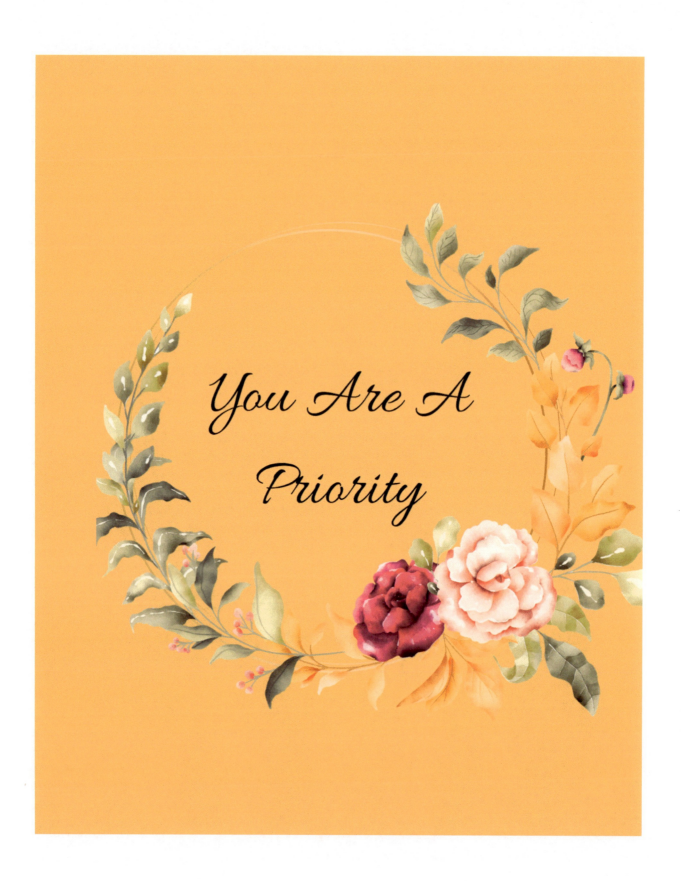

You Are A Priority

You are a priority to yourself. Never put yourself last. It is important to allow yourself to be a priority. There is nothing wrong with placing yourself high on your list of priorities if not first. Have you ever been in the presence of someone who never puts themselves as a priority? They may seem like a very giving person allowing others to overlook or pass them over, while giving the most, but who do you perceive and view that type of person to be? Do they seem to have value to you? Do they seem as if they value themselves? Do the people they interact with seem to place themselves as a priority?

When we place ourselves as a high priority, others follow our example and also place us as a high priority. How you treat yourself is how others learn to treat you. Let me put that another way. You teach others how to treat you by how you treat yourself.

Have you ever witnessed someone who was totally catered to, and treated like they were royalty in a normal setting? For example, have you ever seen a person receive better service or more help and attention because they were well dressed, walked with confidence and looked as if they were a top priority to themselves? This is because that person is sending out information that they are poised, polished, confident and deserve to be treated as royalty. This body language, attention, and effort put into how they look along with confidence in their step says I AM A PRIORITY!

This means whoever interacts with that person is going to receive that message and may subconsciously begin to treat that particular person with more value and as a priority. If you want to be prioritized then you need to first prioritize yourself.

You will start to see how others then begin to prioritize you and treat you like royalty. You will no longer be the witness of how others rush to open a door or be of service to another poised and confident person, instead you can have similar experiences by prioritizing yourself and daily building your confidence level to that of royalty.

Some say that this is conceit or arrogance, yet they never say that about royalty or someone who they themselves prioritize or see as an important figure. They may not see them that way because they feel as if those people have the authority or have earned the right to be confident and seen as a priority to others. In other words, due to their place in society or their reputation, they are seen as someone who is allowed to be arrogant and conceited. Yet those same manners and the same amount of confidence in someone who seems to be an average person, could be a threat to someone who has not yet been able to prioritize themselves in their own life.

Never allow anyone to treat you less than you treat yourself. Do not continue to tolerate their treatment. Simply reject their efforts and treat yourself as a priority and how you expect to be treated by others. Never make exceptions for when a person has shown you they do not see you as a priority. Many people can claim to be treated unfairly due to their place in society and by their race or ethnicity, and many times yes, people are discriminated against for those reasons sadly. Yet, sometimes people discriminate due to how someone carries themselves and how they present themselves publicly.

We need to know that prioritizing our own presentation is how we are purposely choosing to represent ourselves. Does your clothing, hair, nails and level of confidence say that you are a priority to yourself? True, sometimes we have a bad hair day or are in a hurry and we may not prioritize how we look on some days. Still, that is no reason to not prepare in advance ways to prioritize yourself when you are not able to spend more time on your hair or how you look that day. Keep some extra supplies in your car to stay prepared to keep yourself a priority. Keep with you some hair product, a sample size of your signature fragrance and perhaps an extra top in case of a spill or stain. You can customize your own kit of extra selfcare supplies that you keep in your car depending on your needs.

Prepare In Advance

I keep a pair of sunglasses for when I do not have my makeup on. I also have a small first aid kit, and lip gloss. I usually carry a medium to large size purse so most of my supplies are with me. I like to keep make-up, a hairbrush, hair ties, and some form of moisturizer and perfume. If my children need them, I am prepared.

This cuts down on having to purchase these items when in need of them on the go. This also allows you to go to the places you want to go without having to feel as if you are not appropriate. I also recommend keeping a nice cardigan or jacket in your car in case you have to look more pulled together. A pair of nice shoes will complete the look as well. A bag of shoes, and other items you may need will always come in handy if you have a busy schedule.

Treat Yourself

Make sure you try to do something for yourself each day, no matter how your day is going. Take the time to do something you actually want to do. Go someplace you actually want to go. Don't just work or run errands all day and not do anything for yourself. Perhaps you can schedule what you want to do first if you are able to. If not, then at some point during your day, take the time to do so. I like to grab a coffee after I drop the children off to school in the morning sometimes. There is a park that I pass daily that I may go to for the beautiful scenery and nature. Sometimes I just drive around listening to my favorite songs. This is what allows me to feel as if I am a priority to myself.

Balance prioritizing yourself and others

Sometimes we put others before us, due to schedules and times we must complete them, but never feel that those tasks are the priority in your life. They are simply tasks. The people in your life may be a priority to you, just make sure that you are also a priority to them. If you have a small circle of people in your life, this should be easier.

People who run in larger circles may feel that putting themselves as a priority gets challenging at times. I would suggest choosing the most important people in your circle and allow them to prioritize themselves the same way that they prioritize you. You may start to see your circle grow smaller.

Sometimes we don't notice that we are not a priority to those who are a priority to us when we have a larger group of people we interact with. Those relationships can then be modified to the status they deserve, allowing you to see who really prioritizes you more. When you are able to see who puts in more effort and who cares more, you can start to modify your relationships with those people if you feel the same way. If you do not feel the same way, I would suggest showing them your appreciation and telling them how they have made you feel. Telling others that you recognized their efforts, then telling them that your priorities are already in place, may allow them to adjust their own priorities, including you, to their appropriate place.

An example of such a situation would be if someone wants to be your friend and you are not interested in friendship or just don't have enough in common to prioritize a friendship with that particular person. Sometimes when you prioritize yourself you may feel antisocial. If you need to be antisocial for a while in order to keep yourself as a priority, then that's a small price to pay for what you will get in return.

What will you get in return? You may get more time to do the things you want to do, you will enjoy your life a lot more, and you will not feel the obligation to do things you do not want to do for the sake of being social. Have you ever just wanted to relax and do nothing all day, then suddenly someone is calling you for a favor, or to meet up somewhere?

You want to maintain the friendship but also want to relax and do nothing. Your mind then starts to race for an excuse, yet you remember that person did something for you not too long ago, so the obligation for you to do the same starts feeling more like unwanted pressure.

This is one of the issues with being social and trying to maintain relationships you are not going to prioritize. If the person who calls is your family member that you are close with or your child, you would not have to think twice about what you were going to do. This means that in order to have the type of life you want so you can relax and do nothing somedays, you may need to simply not answer your phone.

This could be the best option if you find it hard to say no to people. You can't be bothered if you do not answer the phone. Some people have their phone set to send out an automatic text to the phone calls and texts that go unanswered. "Sorry, I'm unable to answer right now," or "Call you back later." This means you are most likely busy and not able to talk, let alone do any favors or go somewhere that day. Chances are they will text you what they wanted. Then, you can decide when, how and if you want to respond to them, whether it's that day or it's too late to interrupt you doing nothing.

Health and self-prioritization

If you are the type of person who wants to eat healthy, and find it difficult to do so when you are with other people who do not share your same eating habits, and you tend to eat whatever they are eating, then you need to also place yourself and your food choices as a priority. Choose to eat alone or choose to have a meal with them at another time and invite them to a place with a healthier menu. Parents have to resist the urge to eat what their children eat so they can stay healthy. If you are a parent, I am sure you have experienced this. We tend to feel so loved by our children and enjoy having meals with them, that we figure we can indulge more. This is not the best way to feel all of the time.

Stay focused on your health and your personal weight goals if you are trying to maintain your weight and preserve your looks. This is one of the challenges of parenthood. If children see their parents in a healthy lifestyle, they find it easier to maintain their health more. If there is one parent with healthy eating habits and another parent with bad eating habits, the children will be able to see the benefits and the consequences from each parent's choices.

If you are able to get everyone in the household on a healthier diet, this could be beneficial to all, but we know how hard that is sometimes. Balance is better than being too strict with what your family eats. Have some treats and some healthy snacks available. Restrictions from certain foods only make you want them more later on.

Allow yourself to be the example by eating a healthy snack over a sugary one and your children and significant other may follow by your example. Your health is a priority so take care of you.

If you are on the go a lot and a drive thru seems like the only option, choose something small, low in calories and drink water. Try keeping some healthy snacks with you when you are in the car so that you don't get hungry and have to fight the urge of the drive thru choices. Keep a granola bar or fruit in your tote bag so you are able to snack and not have to eat something that you shouldn't. Keeping snacks for your children can also cut down on those drive thru trips when you are in the car. To show your children a more comfortable and luxurious life, allow them to eat while sitting at a table rather than on the go. I know we all have to eat on the go sometimes, but when we do not, we should opt for dining at a table. This will teach them to also spend more time with family. No parents are perfect, so modify your schedule to do what is best for your particular needs.

Summary

- Learn to place yourself as a priority and know if you are a priority to others.
- Know that you deserve to be treated like a priority.
- Treat yourself as a priority though your appearance, eating habits, level of confidence. Prioritize how you accept or don't accept treatment from others.

Next you will learn...

How to use your time in the best way for your comfort and luxury.

Your Own Time

Is Yours

In this section you are going to be using your personal time to create your own life as you choose. You are going to be able to live your dream life with what you already have. You are also going to get more of what you want because you are going to feel as if you have everything you need.

The time you spend on yourself and what you like to do is going to determine how enjoyable your life seems to you at each moment. Do you waste time? Technology and the internet makes it seem like society is wasting time staring at screens all day and missing out on their own lives. I like modern technology and social media as much as the next person, but that is not where I choose to spend my time in order to feel a leveled-up lifestyle of comfort and luxury.

We may enjoy spending time looking at people living their lives and doing what they like to do. But when we do this, we are actually wasting our own time and it's taking away from enjoying our own time that we do have. It is okay to see how others spend their time and choose to live their own lives, if that is what we are also doing.

If we are more focused on others and what they are doing with their time and how they are living, we may not live our own lives to the standards in which we deem as fulfilling and leveled- up.

Be Productive

Give yourself a time limit on how long you spend online. Make sure to give your attention to what you like and what you may see as inspirational and similar to the lifestyle you are creating for yourself. This could mean spending a few minutes looking at outfit ideas or hairstyling tips or even make up looks. Then use what you have learned or what you were inspired by to upgrade your own personal style.

Spend less time viewing gossip and what you don't want to implement into your lifestyle. Start deleting and unfollowing any sort of posts or suggested media that does not improve your lifestyle or does not inspire you to live your own life in a more enjoyable way. It may take a while to get all of those ads and posts off your social media and suggestions, yet the time you spend online becomes more valuable.

When you spend time online, have a mental list of what you are looking for. How do you want to use what you've learned or were inspired by in your near future? For example, when I prepare to go shopping, I may take a few minutes to peek at some outfit suggestions online so that I'm not wasting time roaming aimlessly at the clothing store or in an online clothing store for hours. I know exactly the style and colors I want and I waste less time and spend less money by also looking at the best places to purchase the pieces in the outfits that I want. Then, you can get to the best part of shopping, which is actually wearing the outfit. You can get out of the store faster and get home to wear what you bought or hang it in the closet to wear when you feel like it.

I also do this with any sort of home organizing and crafting projects that I have. I spend a few minutes online getting the information and some ideas on how to implement my vision of how I want to organize and craft. When I have what I need, I get to organizing and crafting. Before I go to purchase anything, I look around my own home to see if I already have what I need or something similar, then I make sure I have the space and the time to start organizing and crafting. There is nothing worse than being excited to start a project and then not having enough time or energy to enjoy the project. While I am researching online for a few minutes, I like to have a coffee or tea and a snack to rev up my energy so that when I am ready to start my project I have the energy I need as well as the ideas and inspiration. I have learned to multitask in order to make the most of the time I have.

Multitasking

Ways to multitask are endless. If you don't have time to read books, listen to audiobooks while driving. Another way to multitask is to go places where you can get more done in one location. I go to a postal service place to drop off my packages for my online store each day. The postal service sells office supplies, makes keys and is conveniently located next to the grocery store and a gas station as well as a few places to grab something to eat. I chose to make my life easier and save more time by going to the post office, then driving to the gas station, then going to the grocery store or looking for a place to grab a quick bite to eat. I purposely chose a postal service next to all the places I frequently need to go to. This saves me so much time, money and gas. Try to implement this sort of planning when running your errands. You save time, energy and get more done.

Running errands may seem like a mundane way to spend your free time, but not when you run errands the way I do. I make sure I look effortlessly elegant if I'm in a hurry to leave the house. When I have more time, I dress and look my best. I like to look well put together and polished depending on where I am going.

You never know who you may see when you are out running those errands. You do not want to see your ex and his new love interest when you are looking your worst. You could remember that moment for a long time and I don't feel you want to spend any time thinking about an ex let alone regretting how you looked when you saw them with his/ her new love interest.

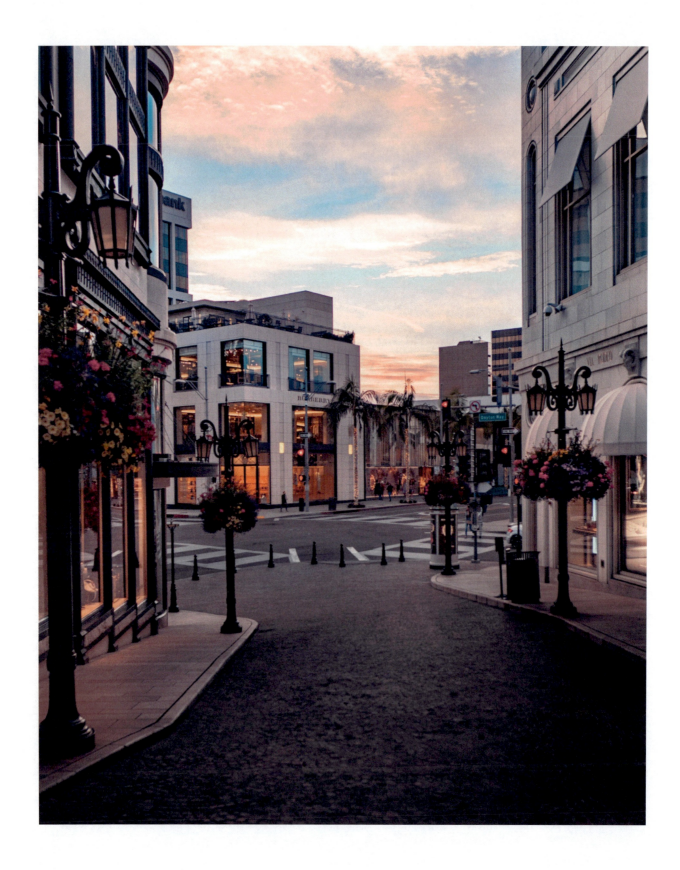

Time can also be spent by doing nothing if that is what you choose to do. Remember it is your time so you may do with it what you please. Never allow someone to tell you how to spend your time. You are an adult and you are able to make your own decisions. If you feel like lounging all day at home, that is your choice. You can lounge all day long and feel as if you accomplished a lot.

Reading a book, listening to music, watching a movie, taking a long bubble bath or just laying down and thinking, these are all ways you choose to relax and put yourself as a priority in ways that allow you to feel comfort and luxury. Earlier in the book I mentioned how to avoid feeling obligated to do something socially when in lounge mode at home, by not answering the phone. If you plan to do nothing all day, do not accept any phone calls that day unless you want to. Allow yourself that time since time is also a luxury. When you live a life of luxury, your time is also part of that luxury so use it wisely on those who you prioritize.

Your time is yours to do with as you please and how you choose to spend it is your choice.

- Create limits on the time you spend online if you tend to waste a lot of time there.
- Multitask and run your errands nearby where there are more conveniences.
- Do nothing and enjoy lounging if that is what you need to do that day.

In the next section you will learn...
How to not care what people think of you.

Staying unbothered is a form of selfcare. When you remain unbothered you remain free and able to live the way you want to live. When we allow certain things to bother us, we are also allowing them to control us to a degree. When we are unbothered, those things or people who are attempting to control us fail. When you do not care what people say or think of you, you control your own life.

Some people make life decisions based on what other people will or do think of them. This could change how you live your life. If someone says your clothes are not stylish or trendy enough, you should not go out and buy trendy clothing. What you can say in a polite way is something along the lines of, "My fashion is classic in style, I can never keep up with the latest trends." This is basically telling that person that you don't care what they think of your style. You will continue to remain unbothered and in classic attire.

If you like trendy and classic styles you could say, "Oh, I only get trendy styles when I feel like it." This takes all the control back as if you have options to dress however you choose without the opinions or suggestions of others. If you find that you are easily bothered by certain situations or people, try to ignore or avoid them. If you are unable to avoid them, simply allow your attention to focus on different situations and people, this way you are not bothered. Sometimes we allow what we dislike to bother us. Many couples who live together could have behaviors or habits that they do not like about each other. They have most likely had these habits most of their lives and find it hard to change. These annoying habits and behaviors could either lead to arguments or suppression of expression due to wanting to keep the peace.

Suppressing your feelings about someone else's behavior is fine for a little while, but eventually they need to know how you feel...

This allows you to have more comfort, luxury and satisfaction in your lifestyle. By allowing yourself to feel unbothered and by keeping the peace, you remain unbothered. You need to stay satisfied in your lifestyle or you may find yourself looking for more when you might not even need more.

Speaking up is also part of staying unbothered. You do not have to speak out of emotion. You can speak and repeat something several times until the message has been received and the issue is no longer an issue. Staying unbothered is almost an art. You have to practice your skills until you are so good at unbotheredness that others ask you how you stay so unbothered. When you know who you are, what you like, what you will accept and what you won't accept, you can easily remain unbothered.

If you find that anyone is bothered by your unbotheredness you know that it is effective. Never allow other people to take this away from you. Staying unbothered is how you are able to continue to feel and live the way you want to. By staying unbothered, you teach others how to stay unbothered so they can feel the way they choose when in a similar situation. When they see you are unbothered, they stop trying to bother you.

If you are the type of person who has anger issues or if you are impatient with others, try taking a break from the issue. You can go outside, or excuse yourself for a moment and do something that makes you feel calm. I like to find a calm comforting song or a movie to watch when I feel that way, or I try to do something creative to express and channel those feelings in a more positive way.

When you are calm, peacfully discuss the issue. Luxury and comfort is also a feeling you give out to others by how you react to them or a situation. When other people can feel comfort and luxury in your presence, by your actions alone, that says a lot. You are going to receive more respect and admiration from others simply by your behavior and reactions to certain situations.

Comfort & Luxury

is also a feeling

Lastly, turn off your WIFI. Yes, turn off your WIFI, including the cameras on all of your apps and the microphones. Use social media and the internet as a tool only. There are ways that these apps and companies try to gather info in order to advertise to you whenever you are online. Some of these ads can even allow you to feel as if your privacy is not private anymore. One way to lessen this and stay unbothered, is to shut off the WIFI when you are not using it, not to mention you sleep so much better when all of those wireless signals are not running through your bedroom and through you. When your info is given to a company they will email you and advertise to you, so if you want to reduce that, try unsubscribing to all the junk mail if you no longer want to get more emails from them.

This helps you to stay unbothered while you are online. You can also have a separate email for those types of websites and apps if you are able to.

Staying unbothered gets easier and easier so try to continue staying unbothered on purpose until it is a natural way of living for you.

I like to take a walk in nature and allow what may bother me to be let go. Walking and breathing in fresh air along with the sounds of nature can help you stay unbothered. You can also write down what bothers you and toss it in the fireplace or burn the paper in a safe place such as a large pot or a BBQ grill outside or if you have a firepit.

Never allow what bothers you to follow you into the next day. Find a way to allow yourself to stay unbothered. Look for solutions and logical ways to solve any issues that you may need to solve. Never see a problem, only see the solutions for the problem and you will remain unbothered because you have the solution to it. Now you must implement it.

Summary

Always look for solutions rather than focusing on the problem or what seems to bother you.

- Staying unbothered is a form of selfcare.
- Take a break from any issue that seems to bother you.
- Learn how to respond to the people who tend to bother you.
- Disconnect from WIFI sometimes in order to limit companies from over advertising or emailing you. This seems to bother many people in this day and age.

In the next section you will learn...

How to spend quality time with those you love and how to make that quality time comfortable and luxurious. I will explain inexpensive and traditional ways to have fun and bond that you can afford. For those who are able to spend, I will also explain several ways how you can bond with others and feel the comforts and luxury in your life.

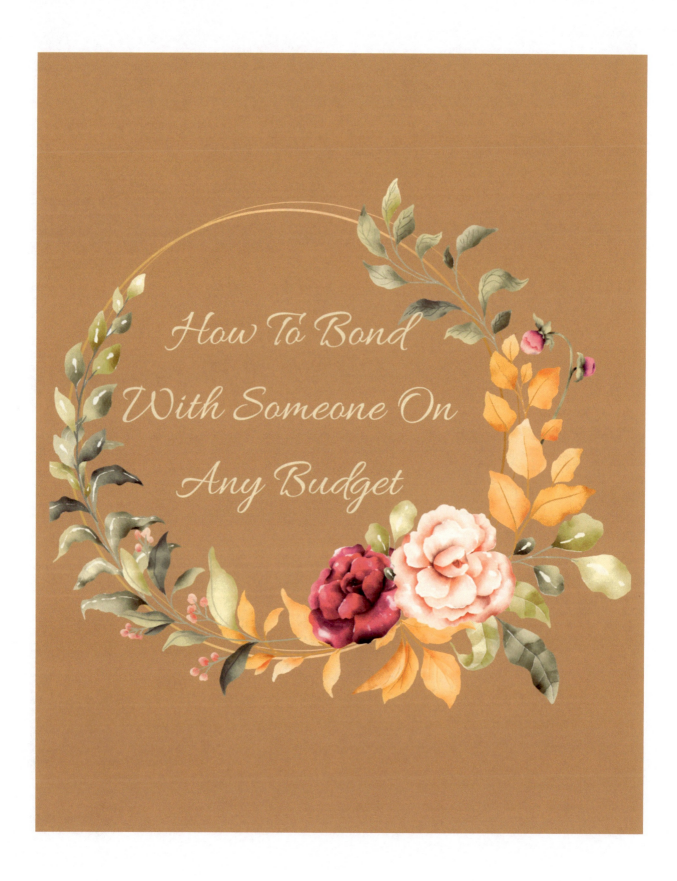

How To Bond With Someone On Any Budget

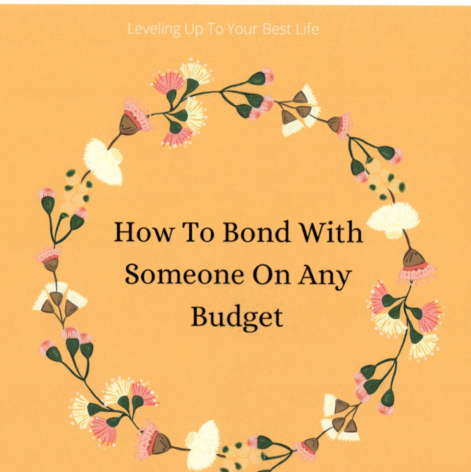

How To Bond With Someone On Any Budget

Bonding with a person is a skill that many of us overlook. In order to bond with someone, you have to spend some time with them. In this chapter I will tell you a few ways to bond with a spouse or significant other, your children, teens, family members, and friends.

Bonding with a spouse or significant other

A few ways to bond with a spouse or a significant other is to first, know some of their favorite activities, foods and the special interests they have. This is important because the bonding is simply the act, yet the gestures and how you are bonding shows how much attention you pay to the them and how you remember. If the person you are bonding with has a favorite meal, prepare it or order out for it. If they have a favorite song or artist, play their music. If they have a favorite drink or dessert, make sure you also have that as well. If they like to dress nice, you also need to dress nicely for them. Bonding over memories that you two have spent together is a fast way to take you back to a time when you may have bonded on a deeper level.

This is helpful when you have been together for a while. This form of bonding can be done at home, on a day trip or evening out depending on your budget and schedules. If you want to make this bonding experience extra special, add some flowers or a gift to the mix. Make sure the gift and flowers have significant meaning for you as a couple. This way the gift will be forever cherished and the flowers will mean even more than just how beautiful they are.

If you have any special talents they like, be sure to implement those skills into your bonding time with them, like singing or playing a musical instrument, for example. If you are an artist and you paint or draw, be sure to show the person some of your latest sketches or paintings that may be inspiring to them.

Bonding allows each of you to know how you value one another and that you want to spend your time with them. With the overwhelming amount of ways to spend our time these days, such as TV, streaming networks, video games and social media, spending some quality time with someone is a comfort and luxury that is most embraced.

Bonding With Children

Bonding with children is a needed activity. With the busy schedules of the parents or the busy schedules of some children depending on their amount of extra- curricular activities, parents and their children need to spend more time bonding.

Children love to eat and make a mess, so one of the best ways I have learned to bond with my children is by cooking or baking something with them several times a week. If you have never cooked with your children or child before, make sure you start off with something they like to eat. I find that a cake or some form of dessert is best. Perhaps have a special apron or a chefs' hat to make the bonding and cooking experience more fun for the children. You can easily order these items online.

This will also allow you to teach your children how to cook so when they are older, they will have some culinary skills along with great memories of bonding over a mixing bowl and a heap of ingredients on the kitchen counter. They may even adopt this form of bonding when they raise their own children in the future.

If you are not one for the kitchen you can bond with your children by means of arts and crafts. Drawing, painting or even molding with clay. Whatever you can make interesting to them is fine.

If you have teens, you could also bond with them in the kitchen or at least over a meal. Teens like to feel as though you are listening to them and know them. They may need some extra bonding time with you as a parent because this will allow them the time to talk about anything that is bothering them or what is going on in their lives. When parents are close to their teens and bond with them often, there is more honesty in that relationship. Always boost their confidence while you are bonding with your children. This will allow for the desire in them to want to bond with you more and they may perhaps suggest some activities to you for future bonding.

If you have a busy schedule and need to plan times to have bonding activities, I suggest a planner where you can plan out activities and places to go together.

You may include the kids in the planning process also if they want to help. This planning journal can also count as bonding if you include them in the planning.

Bonding With Others

Planning activities can also help you keep your promises and your word when suggesting or promising to spend some bonding time with the people in your life. Having a bond with someone is also a way to feel leveled up. This gives you both in the bonding relationship the much needed quality time and communication you need with one another. Talking is the easiest way to bond. Speak to one another on likes, hobbies and things you have in common, focus on the positive when you are bonding with someone.

Make sure the activities you plan include time to talk. Scheduling your bonding time with anyone will automatically teach them to also want to schedule time with you. Your actions and the way you treat others can teach them how to treat you and others they want to bond with.

When bonding with someone in your life, you don't want to emphasize that the time you are spending together is supposed to be for the purpose of bonding. This makes bonding seem like a chore. Instead feel excited to spend some quality time with one another and allow the natural bonding to occur with activities and talking to each other.

If you are not fond of cheap dates, such as walking in a park or getting a coffee, do not accept those types of dates. Instead suggest a classier alternative that is not going to cost too much. You can always get him to spend money later if he likes you, especially if it is a first date.

Normally I do not encourage men to take women on cheap dates, but if you are on a budget or just young without the funds to wine and dine, here are a few Leveled Up Date Ideas.

These ideas will allow you to feel leveled up while allowing your date to save his money for your gifts and bills. Remember this is a SheraSeven book. Haha.

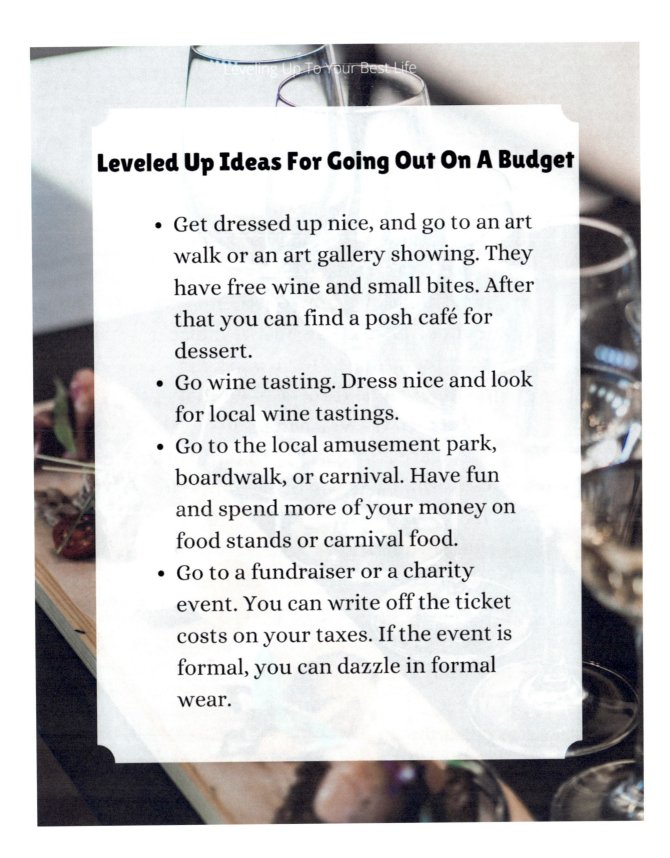

Leveled Up Ideas For Going Out On A Budget

- Get dressed up nice, and go to an art walk or an art gallery showing. They have free wine and small bites. After that you can find a posh café for dessert.
- Go wine tasting. Dress nice and look for local wine tastings.
- Go to the local amusement park, boardwalk, or carnival. Have fun and spend more of your money on food stands or carnival food.
- Go to a fundraiser or a charity event. You can write off the ticket costs on your taxes. If the event is formal, you can dazzle in formal wear.

Leveled Up Ideas For Going Out On A Budget

- Take a cooking or painting class for adults. There is usually wine and time to talk to each other while creating something together.
- Holiday parties can be fun and cost next to nothing. If you work for a company who throws an annual holiday party, you can invite a date. If you are invited to a holiday party by friends, you can bring your date. The evening will be festive, and cost you nothing.
- Grand ceremonies and festivities. Grand openings of new places, ribbon cutting ceremonies, tree lightings, holidays ceremonies, and more. These types of events are usually outdoors and free.

Leveled Up Ideas For Going Out On A Budget

- Farmer's Markets are a fun place to take a date on a weekend morning or afternoon. You can support local small farms and craft makers while spending quality time with someone and maybe buying them some fresh produce and a handmade gift. This type of date costs very little and is somewhat romantic. Your date also has the handmade gift you purchased for them to always remember you by.

- Tours are a way to learn something about the city you live in and its history. In many cities they have historical tours that you can sign up to go to online. Depending on your city and the time of year, you can find some very interesting tours online, from historical tours, all the way to haunted tours if you like those sorts of adventures.

- Horse and carriage rides are not very expensive. It's romantic and a date that will always be remembered. These rides are not very expensive at all and allow you to sit close to each other and feel like royals.

You do not want to accept or take anyone on dates that feel cheap. If you are on a budget you have to think rich while spending less. The mentioned ideas are a few examples. You can come up with some of your own, but be sure those dates do not feel cheap. In my honest opinion, a coffee date is cheap and feels impersonal and unoriginal with little effort. No coffee dates, unless they own the coffee shop. If you are not currently dating or having date nights with anyone, these are also activities you can attend alone or with a friend. When you are living your life and wanting to fully enjoy each day and moment, you never have to spend a lot of money. Luxury and comfort are feelings you have when you are enjoying your time and experience in life in a way that makes you feel as if you have it all.

 If you have never slowed down long enough to simply enjoy your life and make each day a day of comfort and luxury for yourself, try it.

Summary

- You can date/ go out on any budget and have it feel luxurious.
- Memories and experiences are more of a luxury than expensive items or places.
- Originality and thoughtfulness of planning a date does not have to cost a lot to feel lavished and catered to.
- You can also implement all of these ideas with friends or go alone.

In the next chapter, you will learn...
Ways to create luxury and comfort in uncomfortable settings and uncomfortable situations. So many of us overreact or stress out when our lives seem uncomfortable. These uncomfortable times are temporary and can be sailed through with luxury and comfort.

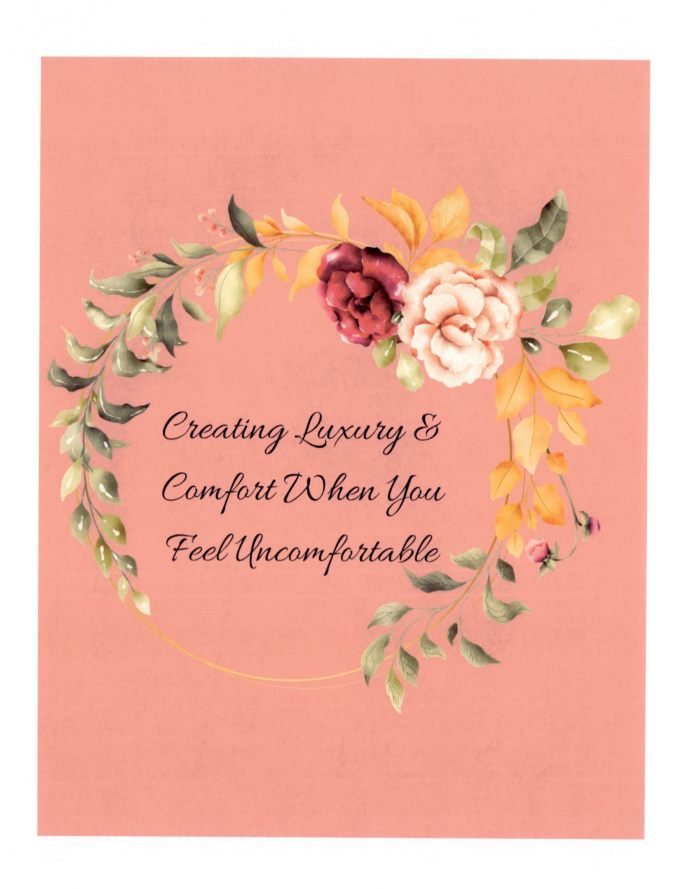

Creating Luxury &
Comfort When You
Feel Uncomfortable

We have all been in uncomfortable situations and we have all survived them. That does not mean we enjoyed those uncomfortable moments. What if I told you that there was a way to actually enjoy the uncomfortable moments? Good news, there is.

If you are experiencing an uncomfortable moment and you want to make that moment luxurious and comfortable, all you have to do is bring luxury and comfort to that situation. For example, if you have to visit someone you do not like visiting, perhaps you can bring your favorite dessert or food and wine to distract you from that person who makes you feel uncomfortable. You can have your visit and sweets, or wine. If you are not a drinker, bring your favorite tea or non -alcoholic beverage. You are practically treating yourself while at the same time making the visit you usually dread so much.

Many people have to attend online or in-person meetings, which can feel uncomfortable, especially if you do not like attending meetings. If you want to make this time seem more luxurious, comfortable and a pleasant experience, bring your favorite items. Yes, bring your most luxurious writing pen and paper, bring your favorite mug or cup that you may sip coffee or tea out of. If you are in an online meeting working from home, create a luxurious ambiance. You can light a scented candle and open the curtains to a nice view. You can put a beach or cozy ambiance on your television screen to create a view if the window view is not comforting or luxurious. Wear what makes you feel luxuriously comfortable while working from home.

Luxury Comfort Kit

If you are in a situation that causes you stress and you want to make that situation more pleasant, try playing some relaxing calming music and brewing a cup of tea while dealing with the issue. There is nothing more soothing and comforting than a cup of tea in a fancy cup. If you are not in the comfort of your own home while having to deal with a stressful situation, always have a luxury comfort kit with you. Yes, you read that correctly, "Luxury Comfort Kit." This is an emergency kit that you can keep in your car, purse, briefcase, or tote bag to always have when you need it. In this kit you should keep the items that bring you the instant feeling of luxury and comfort. A few items you may consider for your "Luxury Comfort Kit" are...

Luxury Comfort Kit

- Your favorite scent, perfume, cologne. A spritz of an expensive fragrance can change how you are feeling and can also remind you of the feelings of comfort and luxury.

- A good quality writing pen. If you are having to sign any documents, take notes or just scribble your stress away, a luxurious pen can also help you feel that feeling of luxury and comfort. This is why many rich and wealthy folks spend money on items such as designer luxury pens. You do not have to spend a month's salary on a designer pen to get the same feeling of luxury. There are replicas and good quality pens in all price ranges. Find a pen that you like to use that feels luxurious to you. This could be the weight of the pen, the flow of the ink, or the look and color of the pen itself. It is also a great item to ask for if someone wants to gift it to you.

Luxury Comfort Kit

- A good coat. The weather can present an uncomfortable situation at times, such as rain, snow, or a windy day. Keep a coat that will always make you feel well put together and one that looks and feels luxurious and comfortable to you. I have a wool pea coat that I like to wear when it's cold. It goes with everything and looks luxurious and best of all it is comfortable and keeps me warm.

- Your favorite treat. Hard candy, mints, trail mix, healthy snacks, or whatever you like that makes you feel comfortable and luxurious. I like to keep a tin of mints. I feel comfortable when I can have minty fresh breath. It's much classier than unwrapping a mint and searching for a place to throw the wrapper. If you are extra classy, you can have a pillbox engraved with your initials and keep any sort of mints in there you like.

Luxury Comfort Kit

- Your favorite lip balm or lipstick. There is nothing like the feeling and comfort of smooth moisturized lips when in a stressful or uncomfortable situation. Keep one of your most luxurious lipsticks or favorite shades of lip color on hand for those times you don't look or feel your best. This will give you a boost of confidence in any uncomfortable situation. Lip balm is also soothing to apply if the fragrance or flavor is comforting to you and your nerves, working sort of like aromatherapy to calm you.

- A book or website full of inspirational quotes. You can stop at any time and read a few quotes to make your situation less stressful and more meaningful. Your entire perspective of the situation could change and the positive just might be seen. You are able to see beyond the situation and perhaps even find a better solution. You may also simply feel empowered and ready to face whatever the day brings.

These are just a few items I recommend, but you can put whatever you like in your own personal "Luxury Comfort Kit."

Your tools are also ways to make unpleasant times seem not so unpleasant. If you like the tools you are using, then you can enjoy whatever it is you are doing. If you have a good laptop, you will enjoy writing more or working online more. If you have high end cosmetics, you will enjoy waking up earlier to apply your makeup so you look and feel more confident that day.

Everyday Luxury Dining

When you have pots and pans you like, you tend to want to cook more and wash the dishes afterwards. It is important we have some of the luxuries and comforts we like to help us perform the tasks we may find unpleasant.

This is why a set of nice pots is an investment in your well-being as well as your ability to feel comfort and luxury while cooking for your family or for yourself instead of it being a task or requirement after a long day.

If you live alone and eat in front of the television daily, this could over time become an unpleasant feeling or situation if you start to realize that you are dining alone and becoming a couch potato.

Set your table and prepare a meal. If you do not cook, order a meal and unpackage it and put that meal on a nice plate. Use real cutlery and glassware as well. Sit and enjoy your luxury and comfort of dining for one. This adds a certain flair of romance to your life even if you are dining alone. It also makes you want to dress better when lounging around your house.

You can bring the feeling of luxury and comfort to your evenings by sitting at a well-set table, playing some ambient music and scenery on the television instead of a show, and adding candle light to your table.

Dining alone does not have to be dreary or depressing, nor does it have to be on a sofa watching reruns or binging a series. You can dine in luxury and style every day.

Dining alone in luxury and comfort may also include inviting someone over or entertaining at your well-set table. The possibilities are open to so many new options that you may have never considered.

Pulling from my own life experience, this book is to help those who want to level up how they feel each day.

Feeling comfortable and confident in your surroundings and environment is important when you want to entertain guests. We also learn to appreciate the efforts and notice the luxuries others provide for us more often and no longer take them for granted.

If you are one of those people who feel that you are not cut out for a luxurious feeling each day, ask yourself why. Why do you feel you do not need or deserve to feel luxury and comfort to bask in daily? Whatever your answer is, I hope that you are able to convince yourself that you indeed deserve to live a life of comfort and luxury.

Luxury Is Beyond Surface Level

If you feel that luxury is something that is only material and superficial, it is not. Some people are uncomfortable with focusing so much on the material world and have guilty feelings for having material things in the world to enjoy.

How can we appreciate and rise to the next level of our being if we never get a chance to feel the comforts and luxuries of such a material world? In the same way we cannot experience the feeling of joy without the feeling of sadness, we need contrast in order to understand the meaning of both and maintain the balance.

Learn to feel comfortable while wearing a satin or silk robe, sitting in a well decorated room, sipping a cup of tea, coffee, or your favorite cool beverage while listening to your favorite music or reading a great book. This is how you should come home to feel after a long day.

When you enter your home, your troubles should feel as if they are melting away.

When you slide out of your shoes and exchange them with something soft and soothing to your feet, you should feel comfort. When you change into your loungewear, you should also feel as confident and luxurious in them as you do in your daily attire.

Your life will always feel as if you are living it on purpose with the intent to make each moment an experience of comfort.

These next sections are going to be filled with some of my experiences and the many ways I have implemented some of these techniques into living my most luxurious and comfortable life at each level since I began living my life on purpose.

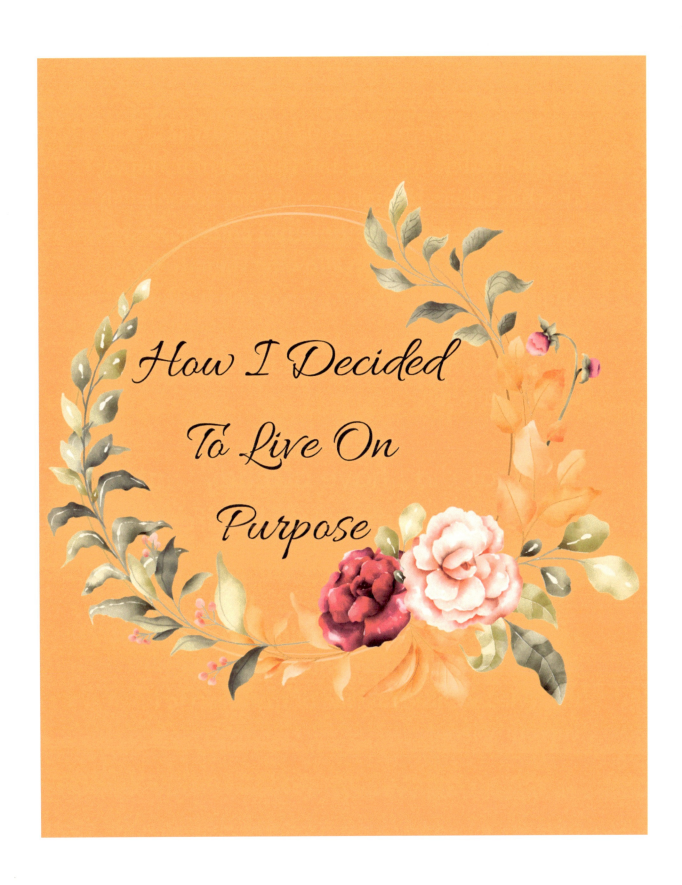

How I Decided To Live On Purpose

I decided to live my life on purpose when people told me I could not. Instead of listening to what others thought I could not accomplish or what lifestyle they thought I could not have, I decided to stop allowing them to try and shape my life the way they felt it should be.

Instead I focused on what I could do with my life at that time.

What did I have already that could vastly improve the lifestyle I was living?

I had nice clothes that I could wear instead of jeans and t-shirts. I would dress for the lifestyle I wanted instead of the lifestyle I currently lived.

Mindful Personal Fashion

I shopped in the nice thrift shops in the fancy areas of town where the quality of the clothing and items were high end. I also caught sales and chose to purchase more classic clothing so they would always remain in style. I did not focus too much on the name brand of the clothing, but the quality of the items I purchased.

Whenever I notice people who I deemed wealthy-looking or who seemed to be enjoying a lifestyle of comfort and luxury, I noticed they were wearing simple yet elegant clothing with very few logos and brand names showing. I noticed they chose simple classic clothing that allowed them to always feel confident in their own skin. You see it was not the clothing that I was focused on when I would notice them, it was their level of comfort, style and confidence.

I decided to give up trendy clothing for that same feeling they exuded. It may be harder for younger people to give up trendy clothing, but when you are ready to live the life of luxury and comfort on purpose, you won't find trends as appealing as you once did. I remember going through my closet and finding the most horrific fashions that had been trendy months before, and now on the clearance racks and "What Not To Wear" fashion blogs. After clearing my closet of these items a few times over the years, I decided to never purchase trendy clothing again. They were a waste of money to me and made any photographs taken while wearing them an embarrassment.

Mindful Eating

The foods I used to eat would also be the sort of lifestyle I would live.

Burgers, fries and soft drinks were not the daily diet of a woman who lived the sort of lifestyle I wanted.

I had to change what I ate. I remember giving up beef and pork in order to not be able to visit a drive thru with ease. This also made it easier to avoid foods high in calories. It was hard at first, and I would have dreams of the foods that I could no longer consume. I had also given up chicken and seafood as well, but I added those meats again after my dreams got so vivid that I could smell food. I simply learned to control the types of foods I was eating and how they were prepared.

Grilled, steamed or sautéed foods were the choice now and fried foods were not on my menu. I noticed that people who looked their healthiest and seemed to be living their best lives hardly indulged in greasy fried food. I had to give that up as well. My drive thru meals were replaced with visits to quaint cafes with fresh items on the menu. Salads and fresh fruit were my new preference. As a result, I lost a lot of weight, my skin improved and my clothing fit so much better.

Why I Chose To Live On Purpose

You may ask what prompted me to make sudden changes in my life, well, it could have been that I was a newly enrolled mortuary student, and suddenly surrounded by death on a daily basis. There is nothing that makes you want to live a better life than to see life at its end regularly. I won't go into the gory details of my life as a mortuary student. Perhaps in another book. Living life on purpose suddenly was something I had to do. I had to stop caring what others thought of me and determine how I would live my life on my own terms. I had to let go of people who were not for my best life as well. I had to suddenly make changes that would allow me to start to live the life I actually wanted to live while I still was able to live it.

life is too short to wait.

If there was someone I wanted to spend time with, I told them. If there was something I wanted to do, I did it. And if I wanted to sing, dance or yell, I did.

Those in life who seemed the happiest, were also the most expressive in their whims and indulged them if they were able to. I believe it was Mark Twain who said, "Dance as if no one is watching." The ability to have fun, not care what others think of you and how you enjoy your life, is one of the keys to living a life of comfort and luxury, because you are comfortable in your own skin. I sang boldly, danced lively and laughed wholeheartedly whenever the opportunity presented itself to do so. Living life with few regrets is a luxury in itself. Never pass on an opportunity to do something while you are able to do so.

I have made mistakes in my life and have made choices that some would say were the wrong ones, yet I never felt that way about those choices. They led me to the life I live today. Some of those choices gave me the confidence I have today and are due to the fact that those choices were major confidence boosters to my self-esteem. There are some people that I have come in contact with in life that I do not know how to thank to this day because they allowed me to see so much more than I had ever noticed before. Living on purpose allows us to feel life on another level that we have not felt before. I have learned to allow that feeling to permeate and seep throughout each day as a comfort to me. This is what living on purpose feels like. Waking up each day excited to see what the day brings and how I will choose to incorporate each moment with the love of the life I have grown to embrace and begin to share.

I don't mean to get all flakey, but when you love life, you see the beauty in all things and you have passion for most endeavors.

It almost seems as if you are in your own romance with life and your daily tasks suddenly include daily encounters with something unseen, yet felt in a way that makes you feel as if you are in a fairy tale, yet still living in reality.

In life we experience major events that change how we feel and think about ourselves. Sometimes we lose ourselves in the situations and the routines of life that have become our daily rituals. We focus on others or on work, and not allow our own lives to be lived the way we had been used to living.

Perspective Is Key

We tend to forget how to live on purpose, and instead live to perform tasks or to please others in some way.

Life is not meant to stay this way nor be lived this way. If you are not living the life you love, then change something. If it is hard to change your circumstance, then change how you feel about your circumstance.

Begin to see the positive and how you can improve your current feelings about what you do not enjoy about life. For example, if you are not happy with your current position or relationship or even how you spend your days, then find a way to do what you love in those moments.

I did not like sitting in line for over 2 hours each day to pick up the kids from school, so I started using that time to read and expand my mind. I also used that time to talk to people who I had no time to speak with otherwise. I also use that time to write. Sitting in line for hours could have seemed like a total waste of time, except I turned it into time to create, learn, brainstorm and write. Sitting in line for most parents may not lead to becoming an author or a well- read life alchemist, but for me it did.

I had some of my happiest moments in the car waiting in line and as a result, I allowed myself to enjoy conversations, books and idea sessions that lead to my current happiness today. And still, I use the time I wait in the car to plan and create.

I decided to use those 2 hours to better my life each day and improve myself. Instead of complaining about the time I spent "waiting," I started loving the time I had to create and to learn new things.

You can choose to live each moment on purpose or you can miss those moments entirely and never use them fully to your advantage.

You Create Your Reality

Life is what you make it, and each moment you are here you are creating your life. You can choose to ignore that and allow life to happen with little influence or you can choose each moment to feel and experience this life on purpose.

How do you want to feel each day? I choose to feel happy and productive each day with successful results and with joy in what I do. That is the life I create on a daily basis and continue to create. I want to also teach others to allow themselves to live their lives on purpose as well. Sometimes we get busy and forget who the author of our story is and we allow our story to stray from where it should be focused and we begin to focus on that instead. You need to be conscious and aware of the influence you have in your own life and use it to live on purpose with the luxuries and comforts you put there and choose to experience by the way you feel.

You must learn to live each day on purpose and to get the most out of life. There are ups and downs, yet you know that you are holding the pen and you are the writer of your own story.

Hands On Luxury
You Make

Hands On Luxury You Make

The myth that luxury is expensive has to end. Luxury simply means "comfort and extravagance." I like to think of luxury as comfort, style and how we feel while enjoying life. Some people actually spend money on trying to feel luxurious with things that they make with their own hands. In this chapter, I will tell you how I made many of my own luxurious products. Have you ever wanted a luxury candle that fragranced a room with the most expensive scent and glowed in the prettiest glass and had an elegant label that screamed "Imported Luxury Candle?" I have. I remember one evening I was online researching the price of a thrifted designer candle I purchased earlier that day that seemed expensive. I wanted to look up the brand of the candle to see if I scored big on a luxury candle for pennies on the dollar. I soon discovered the candle I purchased for ninety-nine cents, had originally cost close to sixty dollars retail. The candle was a luxury brand that was sold in high end department stores. I was thrilled when I saw what a deal I had gotten. I observed the candle and wondered what made a small candle so expensive. I studied the label and the design, and smelled the scent. I saw some fancy lettering. The scent was not a food smell but perfumed with fruity and floral notes that would remind you of a French perfumery.

The candle smelled so expensive and when I burned it, the scent and the flickering glow seemed to somehow transport me to a fancy boutique hotel room with a breathtaking view. In my mind I am transported to a fancy place where I am catered to and my every want and need is waiting to be fulfilled. I remember that feeling and I knew I wanted to have that feeling longer than that designer candle would last.

One rainy day, years after that lucky find of the luxury candle from the thrift store had been burned and discarded, not to mention having moved into a new home, I wanted to recreate that feeling again. I had gone shopping at the dollar store and picked up some square glass jar candles and a few round ones as well. The candles were only lightly scented and not very luxurious in their appearance. I decided to create the look, and scent of a designer luxury candle. Because it was raining that day, it was the perfect weather for a DIY project. I gathered my essential oils and my perfumes, in addition to some stickers I created using shipping labels and my printer. I found some fancy looking labels that looked designer and French-inspired. I printed and cut out the images to fit on the side of the glass candle.

I applied the stickers carefully to the jars and they looked even better than the expensive designer candles. I then poked holes into the top of the candle using a chopstick, to sprinkle in the scented oils and perfume. I used another candle's wax to seal the holes up and just to add a little something extra I sprinkled some fine glitter on top to conceal any evidence of the poked holes. The candle could have sold for at least twenty dollars if I had to put a price on it for retail.

It may have been raining outside but it was bright and cozy inside after lighting the candle I "luxurified." Yes, you read that correctly, I tend to make up words that seem to fit the situation. It is one of the quirky parts of my personality that I have also learned to fully accept and use to feel as if I am some sort of academic wordsmith that obviously has no business creating words!

In this photo are some candles I created using Mod Podge and labels that I directly placed onto the wax. I also used a decorative napkin to "luxurify" the tall pillar candle. I purchased an inexpensive candle and peeled off its label, then I used floral stickers and washi tape to decorate it to match my table scape. I also used an empty food jar and filled it with cotton balls. I placed a floral sticker on the front and sealed it onto the jar with Mod Podge. I housed the jar on the countertop in my bathroom. The candles in the photo were a simple DIY that improved their quality and appearance.

Learn to also enjoy the time you spend creating and crafting the beautiful things you will enhance your home with. Your time and effort will give you much joy, and comfort when you see your creations spread out throughout your home too.

Creating beautiful décor for your home is also relaxing and rewarding. Putting your own creative touches on the bits and baubles that enhance your space is a reward within itself. When you are surrounded with your own creations that actually look good, you not only feel proud of your designs but also comforted by the look of them, not to mention they are great conversation pieces.

I have a beautiful fall hat box decoration that I crafted a few years ago that I still cannot believe I actually created. I still look at it with much satisfaction and it makes me smile. My smile is connected to the memories of making the floral and mini pumpkin bouquet. My daughter and I sat on my bedroom floor and crafted some fall decorations while spending quality mother and daughter time. This Fall hat box will always hold that memory, while being décor that I love.

One evening I was sitting on my sofa and I started to notice how blank my walls were in my dining room and parlor. I wanted to put something on the walls but not just some print or picture with no meaning.

I started to look around my home and I gathered some of the paintings and drawings my daughters had created in their art class at school. I also gathered some of my attempts at painting landscapes, and held them up to the blank wall to see how they would look. I knew that a trip to the thrift store was in my future. I would look through their photos and artwork and find the perfect sized frames. Thrift stores are the best place to find expensive looking frames for only a few dollars. I found a very beautiful framed mirror and some framed floral prints in the thrift store, and grabbed them up as fast as I could.

BEING CRAFTY IS NOT A HOBBY

IT'S A WAY OF LIFE

This is the mirror I found thrifting as well as the beautiful framed painting in the reflection. Most of the items on the mantle were also thrifted, including this elegant candelabra.
The vases were such good finds, I almost could not believe they were sitting on the shelf of a thrift store.

I also found a number of frames for my daughter's paintings. The frames were so fancy and expensive looking, making the paintings look professional. I hung them up in my parlor and dining area.

Feeling comfort and having happy memories while admiring your home décor is the reward you get from taking a hands-on approach to creating luxury for yourself.

Being a naturally creative person, it comes as no surprise that I would have personal artwork displayed. I like to look at the art and smile while feeling a sense of accomplishment. Not only did I create the artwork, but also the art wall decorated with beautifully hung framed pieces. The result is artful décor of my own creativity along with the creativity of my daughters.

The artwork is quite good and deserves to be displayed in a luxurious frame.

Creating hands on luxury can also be a hobby, or a way to spend quality time with yourself, or with others who may enjoy crafting.

If you are a social person, you could invite friends over for a DIY night where you craft beautiful décor items to take home. Sipping margaritas or wine while enjoying each other's company and crafting seems like a fun time and a way to bond. Creating and making lifelong memories with something you can display in your home for years to come can be a good time. Holidays are usually a great time for these sorts of gatherings because more people are in the crafting mood during the holiday season. Not to mention the money you could save by making your own gifts.

This is a hand-held mirror I made. The mirror was purchased from the dollar store. I used pearl beads, a flat glass cabochon with a print of a flower glued on to the cabochon. The mirror was painted with a pale pink acrylic paint to give it a vintage look. A cream ribbon was tied into a bow for the finishing touch.

Selfcare Is The Best Care

Selfcare is a huge part of attaining a sense of comfort and luxury. Remember that luxury is defined as comfort with extravagance. Extravagance can be different for each individual person. For me, extravagance is going all out on something that would normally be deemed as "simple."

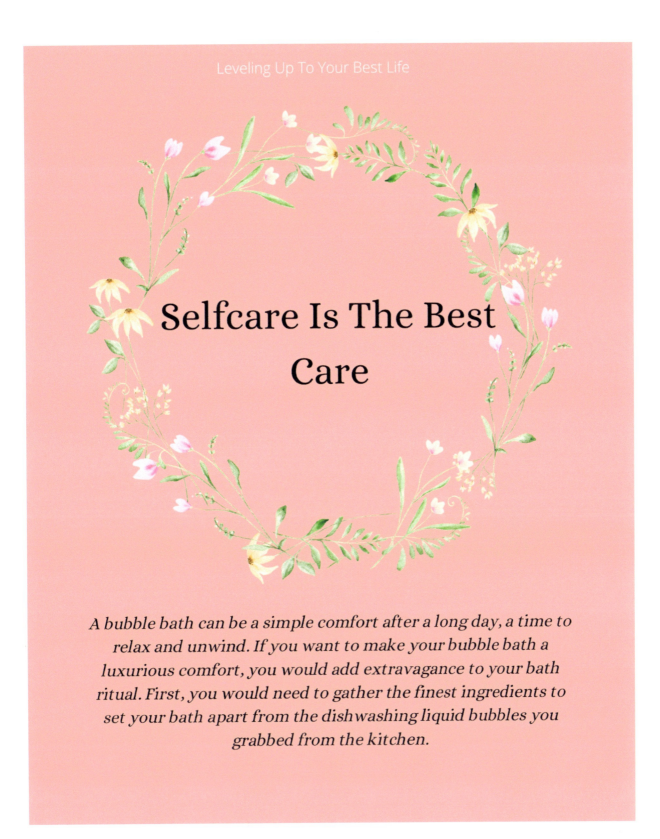

Selfcare Is The Best Care

A bubble bath can be a simple comfort after a long day, a time to relax and unwind. If you want to make your bubble bath a luxurious comfort, you would add extravagance to your bath ritual. First, you would need to gather the finest ingredients to set your bath apart from the dishwashing liquid bubbles you grabbed from the kitchen.

Let's start with the ingredients below:

- Sea salt or Epsom salt
- Lavender or rose essential oils (or oil of choice)
- Luxury bubble bath or shower gel
- Some candles or LED candles for ambiance
- Soothing music of choice, or ambient nature sounds
- Fresh petals or herbs from your garden or bouquet
- Bath bomb in your favorite color
- Sponge or bath poof
- Glass of something to sip on to relax
- A fluffy or silky robe, gown or pajama set to slip into afterwards
- A silky body oil to rub on after your bath
- Cozy slippers
- Clear mind to relax

Sink into the bath with the lights off or dim, allowing the candles to create a soothing relaxing glow. Slip into the bath and allow the scent of the essential oils to fill your senses. Feel the warmth of the water against your skin. Take in the beauty of the petals and herbs that are floating on the water. Notice the color of the water if you chose to add a bath bomb. The soft music helps you drift into the relaxed state that you are sinking into. Your stress eases away slowly and you become aware of your comfort and luxury while soaking away in an extravagant pool of luxurious oils, perfumes and petals.

Sip your wine, tea, or whichever elixir you choose to pour. Allow yourself to enjoy every moment of your bath. Close your eyes and feel what selfcare truly feels like.

Selfcare is more than a physical form of care, it

is a way to appreciate, love who you are and to pamper yourself. It is a way to honor your skin, your muscles and your body. "Take more baths." It seems like that is the answer to so many things. Had a bad day? Take a bubble bath. Getting ready for a big date? Take a soak. Not feeling so well? Take a hot bath. If you are feeling overwhelmed, take a warm bath. A bath is a way to allow the salts, oils, petals and herbs to create an infusion for your body. It's almost medicinal and since your skin is the largest organ, taking care of yourself this way is one of the best forms of self-love you can give.

Make sure to make time each week for your self care. Self-care is also a time for reflection and to replenish. Taking a day off and reading a good book is also a form of self-care if you ever feel overwhelmed by your normal schedule.

Making time to do what you feel most relaxed doing is very important. You never want to get to a place in your life where you phase out the relaxing ways you spend your time. This will lead to more stress and less rest.

Rest is an important part of life. We tend to stay so busy that we forget that rest is the way we replenish and continue being our best selves. I feel that society has us competing with each other and we forget that we only need to compete with ourselves. We know our own needs and wants including when we need to rest and when we want to have fun.

Don't Forget To Have Fun

Having fun is another form of self-care and we need to embrace the fun in life more often. One of my fondest memories in life is of me having fun.

Amusement parks, roller coasters and vacations hold some of the most valuable memories and fun times, which is why we need more of these memories. Try making time for mini vacations if you are unable to get away for a long vacation. A weekend trip is very refreshing and can be super replenishing to the soul. Having a fun weekend is also a way to not burn out at work. If you do not work, mini vacations also allow you to experience variety in your daily, weekly and monthly routine and it breaks up the monotony of your day to day schedule.

Alone Time And Saying No

Being alone sometimes is also another form of self-care. The pressure of always having to meet up with someone or call them can be daunting. When our schedule is clear and no one is expecting anything at all from us, there is a weight lifted and a feeling of freedom like no other. Never be afraid to cancel plans or make plans if you know you won't feel up to meeting anyone. It is better to avoid a situation you are not going to enjoy. Some people have a problem telling others no when they are invited to a function or when asked to help with a task. Just remember that "No." is a complete sentence. That means you never have to explain yourself and the word "No." should be enough.

Map Out Your Time

If you are polite, you can say something along the lines of, "I'm not going to be able to make it," or "I have prior plans." No one has to know that your plans include lounging on the sofa reading a book. Your time is your time. If you need to map out your time for the things you want to do, including time for self-care, I suggest using a planner. I have several planners and I like to write down how I want to spend my time. I would not call it a schedule, but a map of how I plan or hope to spend my time. I do not like the confines of a schedule in a planner. If I see it as a schedule to keep or some sort of to-do list, I may tend to avoid it.

If I don't get to the plans in the planner it is no big deal and can be moved to a later date.

There should never be a feeling of pressure when you plan.

If I start feeling pressure when I read my planner, I stop using it for a few days or so. This is simply to allow myself to not feel the pressure or need to complete any tasks unless I want to. Having this sense of freedom allows me to enjoy doing those things I need to complete. I suggest planning tasks way ahead of time to give yourself plenty of time to complete them or reschedule them if you feel like you are not up to it that day.

I have looked back in my planners from the past and there are tasks from last year that I am just now completing. Those tasks never had a deadline, they were just things I wanted to find the time to do someday. No sense of urgency whatsoever, and it turns out that a year later was actually perfect timing for those tasks to be completed. Turns out I had more inspiration, time and energy to actually enjoy the tasks, complete them and have them turn out a success.

My planners each have a different task. I have one planner for goals and manifesting, one for appointments and daily tasks, and another for enjoyment.

The planner I use for goals and manifesting has motivational quotes, a place to write my goals for the week, and how I plan on completing them. I tend to choose easy goals that are not so hard to complete that eventually lead to bigger goals. For example, if one of my goals is to eat healthy, that small daily goal will most likely result in a healthy life and maintaining my weight. I also use that planner to set aside time to write or be creative in some way. The planner I use for appointments and daily tasks is just to make sure I have a record of the things I need to keep track of, such as when certain things are due, or reminders of places I need to be for the kids. That planner is usually kept with me or also used as a visual reminder of what I have

probably already added to my calendar on my phone.

The planner I use for enjoyment is decorated with all sorts of stickers and drawings, quotes that inspire me and plans for fun things to do. I also like to keep track of cool websites and ideas to research for future enjoyment. If there is a new eatery I want to try, I will write down the location and when it would be a good time to visit. I also like to decorate that planner according to the seasons and have fun decorating the pages. I like to look at it as sort of a planning scrapbook.

I also keep my planners so that I can look back at them years later, like a journal, except I have dates, events and cute stickers to tell a story. I also keep journals as well, with a more detailed account of what occurred on certain dates.

I do not write in them daily, just when I feel the need to document what I am feeling or an event that occurred.

I also use planning and journaling as a form of creative release. Being creative is also a way to express your feelings about your life and how you are living each day on purpose. You can actually see how much you are enjoying your own life and how you fill each day with meaningful ways to experience it.

These types of planners and journals can also help you if you feel like you are in a rut. You can flip back to more fulfilling times to see what you were doing and maybe revisit some of those activities and plans that were the most exciting to you. I have glanced back and reminded myself of fun activities to do on the weekends such as farmer's markets, carnivals, and certain festivals I had forgotten about that happen annually. Reminding yourself of how to live on purpose is also a major part of self-care.

Food

Food is a major part of living life on purpose and enjoyment. Make sure you are not using food to fill your voids, but to enjoy your life. As mentioned earlier in the book, place settings and dining on a set table is part of enjoying the meals you prepare at home.

I feel that eating at a set table makes food taste better and you actually enjoy it more. Food can alter the way we feel about life. Fresh fruit makes me feel like there is a newness or freshness to life and that there is so much to experience. A warm bowl of soup allows me to feel like there are many comforts in life that we should never take for granted.

A spicy dish gives me the feeling of adventure and the need to seek out more. A crisp salad gives the feeling of health and vitality, youthfulness and a reminder to stay healthy and balanced.

Foods can offer you the chance to make memories over cooking and bonding and sharing a meal with special people. Which is why most holidays are spent cooking and spending time with friends and families gathered at tables. We don't always need a special holiday to invite people over for a meal. It is a way to show love and appreciation to others in your life.

Food can be used in so many ways that enhance the quality of each day. People have used food for celebrating, comforting, gifting and healing. We can do so much with food to make each day exceptional.

When I was younger I went to culinary school. I actually have a degree in culinary arts. Food is a major part of our lives since we need it to survive.

Why eat the same old boring foods when you can explore new cuisines and ways of cooking. Some people never get to experience the variety of cuisines that are available because they weren't exposed to them, where they were raised, and their cultures. I remember the first time I tried Thai food. I was hooked. I could not believe I had gone most of my life never having tried this spicy exotic cuisine. Thai food quickly became one of my top two favorite foods to eat. I can go out to lunch by myself and go to a Thai restaurant and never notice that I'm alone, because the food is so good. I may not even remember to talk or socialize with anyone if I have company because I am so focused on the food.

Finding a favorite cuisine can bring purpose to your day, even on a mundane day when you have nothing to do.

You can get dressed and take yourself out to eat. Food can also allow you to be creative especially if you are learning to cook a new dish. It gives you a sense of accomplishment in your day, if your days are not very eventful.

Make sure you are cooking something that you can be proud of, such as a cake, pie or some dish you have never cooked before. I remember the first time I baked a loaf of bread. I felt like I had performed some sort of miracle. I always thought baking bread was a talent that only the most skilled people could do. Even in culinary school they left the bread baking towards the end of the semester. Having all the professional tools at culinary school was helpful, but the first time I made fresh homemade bread, I added too much salt and it looked ugly. Yes, I was still proud of my ugly looking salty bread, because it was still bread and it was edible. I can still smell the aroma of that bread.

I have improved a lot since then and have made more successful loaves of bread that were delicious, but the memory of that first homemade loaf will always remain. Food tends to provide us with memories laced with delectable smells and nostalgia as well as a sense of comfort.

If you are not good at cooking there are meal subscriptions that come with instructions and online videos on how to prepare them. The ingredients are already pre-measured and prepared to cook. It's also a feeling of taking care of yourself that gives you a sense of self love. When you have no idea what to bring someone for a gift, food is always a good option. You can choose to give them a gift card to their favorite place to eat, or a basket filled with their favorite snacks and treats. The person will think of you as they indulge in the tasty gift you provided. Food serves as a way to get to know others, especially if you are dating and dining out with a new acquaintance. When we think of the perfect meal to order on a first date, it is customary not to order spaghetti or anything that can stain our clothing, yet as we get more comfortable with the person we are dining with, we will order whatever we are in the mood for.

Food allows us to express ourselves when we are starting to feel comfortable around someone we are seeing.

It is a way to indicate that you are not afraid to show your real appetite. Here are a few of my favorite recipes.

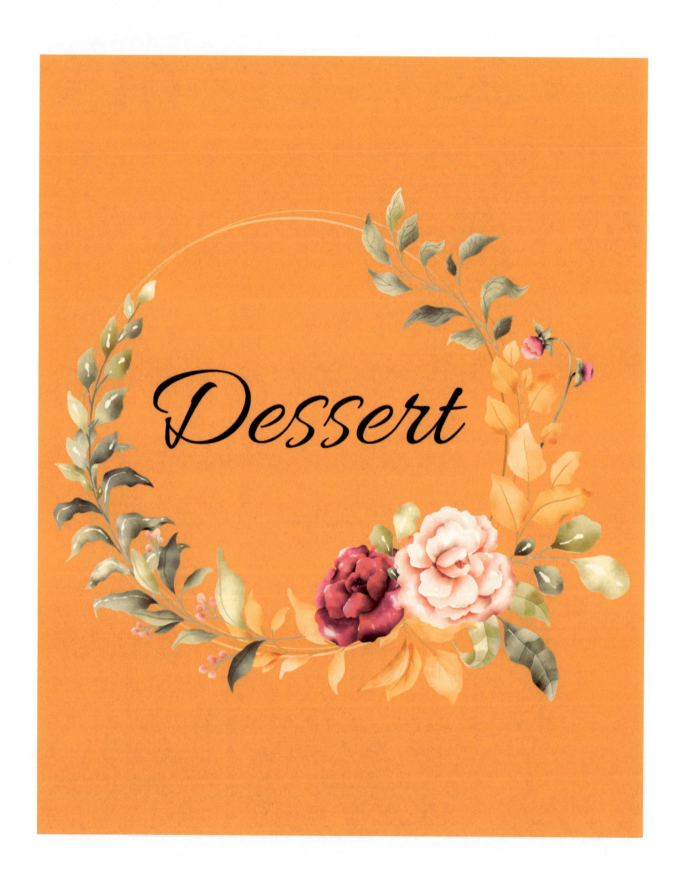

Dessert

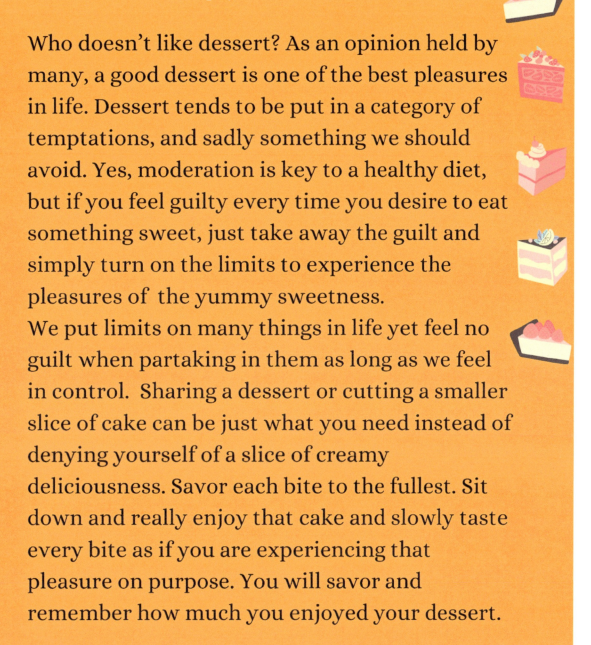

Who doesn't like dessert? As an opinion held by many, a good dessert is one of the best pleasures in life. Dessert tends to be put in a category of temptations, and sadly something we should avoid. Yes, moderation is key to a healthy diet, but if you feel guilty every time you desire to eat something sweet, just take away the guilt and simply turn on the limits to experience the pleasures of the yummy sweetness.

We put limits on many things in life yet feel no guilt when partaking in them as long as we feel in control. Sharing a dessert or cutting a smaller slice of cake can be just what you need instead of denying yourself of a slice of creamy deliciousness. Savor each bite to the fullest. Sit down and really enjoy that cake and slowly taste every bite as if you are experiencing that pleasure on purpose. You will savor and remember how much you enjoyed your dessert.

What is your favorite dessert? How many times have you felt guilty for eating something that should bring you joy? Perhaps it's time to experience dessert in a new and better way. We tend to feel better about eating desserts and sweets during holidays and celebrations. We eat them and enjoy them to the fullest.

In the moment, we are happy and comforted by the seasons and celebrations that are happening. Then, on the first of the year, all the guilt of holiday eating is suddenly turned into what may be called, "New Year's Resolutions." My solution to food guilt resolutions are simply to enjoy the food, limit the amount, and allow yourself to celebrate life when the opportunity is presented. One way I have learned to limit my cravings while enjoying them is to allow myself to have dessert if I want it, and to prepare the desserts myself. Making cakes, pies, cookies, and other sweets can be a great way to creatively express yourself while also making something that others can also enjoy.

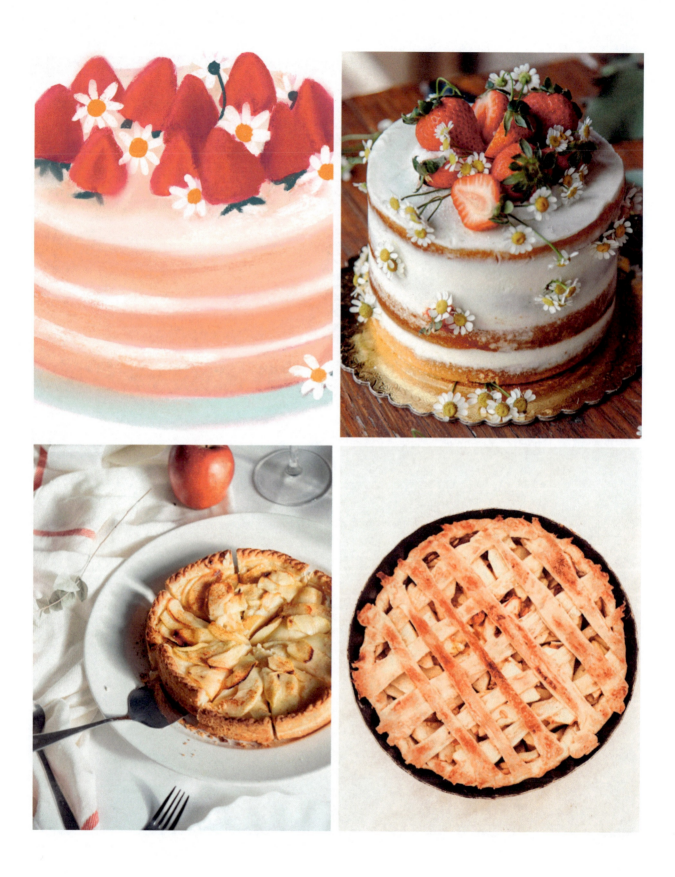

The Perfect Apple Pie Filling

Ingredients:

- 7 sliced apples peeled
- 1/8 tsp of cloves
- ¾ cups sugar
- ½ tsp of nutmeg
- 2 tbsp of flour
- Pinch of ginger
- 1 tsp of cinnamon
- Dash of Salt
- 1/8 tsp allspice
- 2 tbsp butter/vegan butter
- 1 Tbsp of lemon juice
- Cinnamon & sugar to top crust
- Store bought refrigerated Pie Crust or make your own from scratch)

Instructions:

1. Preheat the oven to 400 degrees.
2. Combine sugar, flour, salt and spices. Mix into the sliced apples.
3. Place pie crust over the pie plate dish. If not lattice crust add slits for steam to escape.
4. Fill pie plate with apple filling and pats of butter.
5. Add on top crust and sprinkle with cinnamon and sugar
6. Cover edges of pie crust with aluminum foil.
7. Bake in the oven for 45 to 50 minutes.

Pie Crust

Ingredients:

- 1 ¼ cups all-purpose flour (150 grams)
- ¼ teaspoon fine sea salt
- 10 tablespoons unsalted butter/vegan butter, cold and cut into cubes
- 2 to 4 tablespoons ice water, as needed

Instructions:

1. Mix all the dry ingredients together.
2. Add the butter. For vegan butter, make sure it is chilled or out of the freezer.
3. Add water to the dry ingredients, then stir with a spatula and knead the dough with flour dusted hands until it turns to a dough-like consistency.
4. Use flour to coat a flat cool surface and then roll out the dough with a rolling pin to desired thickness for a pie crust.
5. Cut the dough into strips for lattice crust (criss-cross pattern). Or cut a few slots for a more crust covered pie.
6. Put in the refrigerator or freezer before cutting the dough to keep it firm.

You don't have to wait for a special occasion or holiday to celebrate life. You can make a special meal and sip from crystal glasses whenever you choose to. As I mentioned earlier, you can purchase fine china and stemware at antique shops and thrift stores if you are on a budget. I actually prefer to buy my china from these sorts of places because they will be unique and more valuable. If the dishes you find are no longer produced, then you have found a rare, unique and most likely valuable set of china.

There are markings on the bottoms of most dishes that you can research to find their value. You will see a lot of these antique and vintage dishes for sale in online stores such as Ebay, Etsy, and other places.

One day I was shopping at my local thrift store and I found a pair of coffee mugs that looked like a pattern I'd seen online in a tablescape video. I quickly grabbed the mugs and put them into my shopping cart with a special feeling of glee inside from the sheer luck of finding a very good brand of earthenware. I researched the brand of the mugs and learned their value. These sort of mugs sold online for at least thirty dollars each. I had gotten them for only two dollars a piece.

This is the very reason that I enjoy shopping in thrift and antique stores. The thrill of a deal is a feeling like no other. It's almost like finding valuable treasures.

I celebrate these sorts of finds. I also love to decorate with such items in my home because it makes me feel like I have so much more than I had to pay for. And the items may even increase in value too.

It was my mother who introduced me to thrift shopping. I can remember as a teenager going to thrift stores with her. We were not poor, but she had a resale shop attached to another business she owned and she would supply a lot of the items she sold there from local thrift stores. My mother was always thinking of ways to make money. I learned so much from her. She found so many treasures and valuable items that she sold for much more than she paid for them. She also saved so much money on decorating her other business next door using thrifted items such as furniture and other fixtures. This is probably why I tend to do the same even though I have the money to shop for brand new items, I still enjoy the thrill of finding a treasure, saving money and having something completely unique.

I celebrate the little things in life as well as the big things. I allow myself to feel happy for so many different reasons. Some people try to put a limit on the things you can celebrate or feel happy about, but I like to see just how many things in one day I can celebrate and feel happy about. Why limit your amount of happiness and celebration when you can enjoy each day to the fullest?

Celebrate The Mundane

Why are we saving our ability to be happy and celebrate only at certain times? The times when we are just sitting down watching TV and not really doing much, is an opportunity to celebrate. Give yourself permission to make yourself even happier than circumstances may seem at the moment. Instead of choosing a movie to watch, you could instead choose a theme. You can choose a period movie, a comedy, horror, or an action adventure movie to create a theme and really get into character or at least the wardrobe.

Speak in an accent or even prepare a meal that may be in the theme of the movie. Movie night in this way, becomes a whole event. If you are the social type, you could even invite people over for a night of cocktails, dinner, and entertainment in the theme of your choice. Not all dinner parties have to be about dinner, they too can include a theme.

I am always looking for a way to make life more interesting, entertaining and a reason to celebrate.

Celebrating normal, everyday things can also create more fond memories where they may usually have been less memorable occasions. Such themes can also be the reason for more photo opportunities. Those memories will naturally be preserved by not only you, but also by those who you invited to join you.

My sister is great at throwing themed events and celebrating life to the fullest. She is the one who taught me to do the same. I probably do not celebrate on the same scale as she does, but I learned that it is perfectly fine to celebrate when one feels like celebrating. No need to wait for a special holiday. Simply celebrate because you choose to.

My sister and I share the same date for our birthdays except she is a little older. I was born on her birthday when she was eight years old. I bet that put a damper on her celebrations, which is why I believe she celebrates more than anyone I know, and with good reason. I am not sure how I would feel if I had to share a birthday with someone much more adorable and cuter than me as an eight year old for many years to come. When I got old enough we started to have fun celebrating our special day together with lavished themed parties.

One of the best parties I have ever been to was thrown by my sister. It was a formal masquerade party. She had gone all out. She even hired a belly dancer, a DJ and an MC. The hotel where the party was held was also very nice. I was so glad to have been a part of the celebration.

My sister does not wait around for others to invite her to parties or places, she simply creates what she wants to experience and then invites others to her experience. I feel that she has taught me to be creative in that way on a different level.

I make it a point to surround myself with all the things, and people that I like. Life is meant to be enjoyed and if you have the ability to make yourself feel good, joyous, and fulfilled most of the time, then life is full of bliss. Most of the time I am surrounded by a collection of my favorite items.

Surround yourself with what you really enjoy doing or what you like to look at. I usually have a cup of tea, a book, a journal, my phone, cozy slippers and a nice blanket or robe. If I am not lounging, I usually have on an outfit that makes me feel good about myself, my makeup done, and a planner with what I intend to do that day. I also always leave space for being spontaneous.

I like to eat a meal at a set table and enjoy whatever I am eating, even if it is takeout. I celebrate by showing myself how much I am worth and how I deserve to live the life that I am capable of living. Lately, I have been into gardening. Starting a few raised garden beds in the backyard has allowed me to really celebrate the small things. When I see a new rose bud starting to open, I feel excited. When I see the large green leaves on the kale that I planted get larger each day, I feel so happy.

We tend to look past all the small celebrations of nature and only to celebrate the calendar marked occasions or big news. Why wait when you can celebrate those intricate, more intimate things that you so much enjoy daily? I prefer to live like this every day.

They say to never save your good dishes for special occasions, or your nice dress for going someplace grand. Wear it now and eat off of those expensive plates today. Just be sure to wash them carefully. We also learn to appreciate all that we have earned and worked for a lot more if we are able to enjoy the fruits of our labor. Those fruits could represent giving yourself permission to live lavishly with all the things you were saving for a special occasion. Put on your best dress, set your table, light those candles, play those records, and get the good wine out. Live and love your life as a person who knows how to actually enjoy the level of life they are living.

As I mentioned earlier in the book, you can have a beautifully set table without spending a lot of money, you just have to know where and how to shop. Thrift and discount stores are your friends when wanting to create your luxurious environment for a fraction of the cost.

Celebrate Learning

Celebrate gaining new knowledge and learning new things that better your life. I feel that people do not celebrate what they have learned enough. Many people may not share the same interests as you or like the same things as you like or have studied what you have, but that is no reason not to celebrate how that particular interest of knowledge makes you feel. Many people use social media for this purpose, to celebrate and share with the world how much they have learned or some of their hobbies. Celebrating can look like so many things today.

Some people even make groups, clubs and more to celebrate shared knowledge and interests. To me this is all a form of celebration. You don't have to make a big deal every time you want to celebrate something meaningful to you unless you want to. It can be as simple as a toast or a post. You can even write about it in a journal and mark the date in your planner or calendar.

If you are celebrating the small but meaningful things in your life, your mood is much better. Your life starts having more meaning and you are able to look forward to each day as something to celebrate just because.

Protect Your Bliss

Protect Your Bliss

Protect your bliss. This is important and necessary. Protecting your bliss means protecting your well-being and your leveled-up lifestyle. People will try to steal your bliss and distract you from living your best life. Just know that you and only you have the authority to allow them to do so. If you are not in the mood to hear what they are talking about, especially if it is negative or hurtful, you can dismiss them, or excuse yourself from their presence in order to keep your bliss.

Many people do not have the mindset to live their best lives with their own comforts and luxury that they can afford. No one ever showed them how or explained to them how it can be done, so they may still be searching for their bliss and unable to find it. They may want to take yours from you in order to feel that their lives are not so bad. If you are a kind and caring person you could share some of your ways with others to help them achieve their bliss and to live their best lives. If the person is too negative or you feel it will be a waste of time, you have the right to leave their presence. Keep your bliss and your peace as a priority and you will continue to thrive and live your most luxurious and comfortable life, on any budget.

Write down and journal all of the encounters you experience with people looking for their own bliss. They may express this in a negative way as I explained above, and if they are someone you know personally such as a family member, a co-worker or an acquaintance, be sure to make notes of what it is that triggers their negative attitude. You may be able to help them find their bliss the next time you are able to speak with them when they are in a more positive mood.

Money Alone Does Not Create Bliss

You cannot allow anyone to continuously target you if they are not happy with their lives. You either have to point them in the right direction or allow them the pleasure of your absence. If you have one dollar or one billion dollars, you can still lack bliss in your life. So many people are not able to fully enjoy the money they have earned or the money they continue to make because money does not create bliss. How you use that money can help you to find your bliss. How you live your life in addition to the money you have can vary.

A person with a large bank account may seem to have it all, yet cannot find their bliss. While a person with less may seem to be living a richer, more fulfilling life than a person with more funds. This has nothing to do with the amount of money you have, it is about how you spend your time and energy each day living the life you actually want to live. If you are too busy with business or work and you want to paint, or draw, and do all the things in life that actually bring you happiness and joy, but never allow yourself the time, then all the money you have, is not the answer.

Find
your
bliss

Enjoy Yourself At Work

You must take control of your life and make it how you want it.

You can work, but take breaks. You can focus on business but perhaps in a more creative way that allows you to do some of the things you enjoy. For example, if you like gardens or art, why not hold your next big meeting in an art museum conference room? How about a working lunch in a hotel with a lush garden in their courtyard? If I were the head of a large company I would have all sorts of fun and interesting places to "work." I feel that work should be enjoyable for everyone, and if your work is not part of your bliss, you should reconsider how you work.

Due to the many changes the world has recently gone through, many people now have the privilege of working from home and can make "work" more structured to how they want to live.

As I mentioned earlier I have raised bed gardens in my backyard, and I run my business out of my home, so when I take a break, I simply walk outside to tend to my garden, or just relax outside for a few minutes to enjoy the view with some music and a beverage. I celebrate the bliss that exists from having so many ways to enjoy life in my own environment.

I'm never focused on what I do not have or what I cannot do because I have created my environment and the life where I am able to have and do what I want. This does not mean I have everything, it means I have everything I want. You also have to remember that at some point in your life, you wanted exactly what you now have, so enjoy it and find ways to live your best life at the level you are currently at.

Know How To Uplift Yourself

Sometimes you have to protect your bliss from your own thoughts. Whether they are negative, self-defeating, or just distracting you from your goal, it is also important.

Switch up your mood instantly by throwing on your favorite music, or watching your favorite movie that is uplifting. I know that when I start to feel a certain way, I put on my old albums and allow myself to drift and think of a much simpler time and how great the music is. The nostalgia of a time when life was lived on purpose.

Music
I have a few Ella Fitzgerald albums I like to listen to when I am journaling or taking a bubble bath. I like how romantic and feminine her music makes me feel. I also listen to Billie Holiday while gardening and spending time outdoors in my backyard. It is a nice jazzy classical style of music that adds to my bliss. Some would say she was a blues singer as well, but compared to the music of today, her blues are no longer considered negative, she is simply expressing her feelings.
I also like to listen to her when I am writing, which leads me to another way to protect your bliss- having a playlist of music to play for certain occasions.

You can have a relaxing music playlist, a self care playlist, a gardening playlist, a workout playlist. Many people make daunting tasks entertaining, fun and blissful by adding music.

I know when some people clean they like to play music.
I like to play music when I cook sometimes. It feels like I am being creative and living on purpose while preparing the food. I also like to cook with my daughters and teach them at the same time about preparing food and good music. I know my taste in music has rubbed off on my youngest, and my passion for preparing good tasting plant-based food, has rubbed off on my oldest daughter.

Day Trips

A day trip is the perfect way to refresh yourself from day to day tasks. You do not have to travel very far at all. You simply need to take the time to go exactly where you want to go. Do you want to go antiquing all day and not have to worry about anything else? Then plan to do so and go have your day trip antiquing in your own town.

A day trip can also be an adventure with someone special, a friend, family or a social group. It is all about what you want to do and how you want to spend your time.

One of the best things about working from home or remote, is that you can go anywhere, as long as you are able to connect to the internet and check in at work when you have to. There are some cute boutique hotels and Bed and Breakfast Inns, where you can vacation and still work.

A day trip can also be a needed vacation. It is very important to have fun in life and keep balance. I work for myself but it is still easy to work long hours and forget to have fun, especially when you enjoy what you do. Many people really love what they do for a living and feel as if they are not really working and forget to take breaks. Some people feel that a break is needed, but I say if you are able to balance, live your best life on purpose and enjoy what you do, then you deserve a day trip, a vacation, prosperity and much more.

I have taken day trips to the mall, to the high-end cosmetic stores, thrift stores, to the movie theater, to have tea and so many more fun activities.

I also do not mind going on a day trip alone. I enjoy spending time alone, going and doing everything I like with no compromising. It is simply what I want to be doing, no questions asked. This is important, especially if you have a family or live with someone. Sometimes you need that alone time to really keep yourself authentic to the things you enjoy and like without having to make compromises with anyone else.

Play Dress Up

You are never too old to play dress up. If you think that you are, then you do not know what you have been missing. Many adults tend to use themed parties or holidays to play dress up, but you can play dress up whenever you want. Playing dress up does not have to consist of gaudy costumes or strange clothing. You can dress up according to the theme of how you are feeling that day. If you are feeling like you want to read a book and drink tea by the fire all day long, dress for the occasion.

Perhaps you can draw inspiration from one of your favorite characters in a book or a movie that you might have seen. You might grab a cozy sweater, a long skirt or pair of slacks, reading glasses, a argyle socks and loafers. Light your fire, grab your books and brew your tea. You are now dressed up for the occasion to read and sip tea by the fire. Another way to play dress up is to dress in a certain era. If you are currently enjoying a television series or book set in a period of time that you wish you could have lived in, why not create an outfit inspired by that time period?

I enjoy films and books that are set in the Victorian and Edwardian eras, so I incorporate lots of lace, long skirts, ankle boots, vests, corsets, gloves, and hats. You can modernize your look with less structured clothing by pairing a long skirt with a fitted lace blouse and a pair of ankle boots with a fitted vest that buttons and serves the same structure as a corset. You could also try a dress with a fitted bodice and puffed sleeves for a more country living look from those eras.

You will still have your modern clothing, yet they will be reminiscent of the eras you like. Another way I like to play dress up is to have the proper attire for certain activities. For gardening, I have a pair of overalls, a straw hat with a lace bow, a pair of gardening clogs and some cute gardening gloves. I feel like I am dressed for the occasion and therefore I enjoy gardening even more.

Yes, I am an adult who still plays dress up to have fun and enjoy life. You can do the same. On a hot summer day, put on a cute pastel colored dress, a pair of sandals and sunglasses, and head to your local ice cream parlor for a scoop of your favorite flavor.

If you are going thrifting, put together a boho look of eclectic pieces you probably found while thrifting. There is no reason you cannot dress for each occasion in life to make life the way you want it.

Each morning before I get dressed for the day, I think about what my plans are, and what occasion I should get dressed for. I usually opt for something appropriate for the day's activity. On some days I change clothes at least 3 times. If I want to go for a walk in the park, I dress for the weather and ability to move freely. When I get home I may change into my gardening outfit if I plan to plant some seeds or water the garden. After I am done gardening, and I plan on going anywhere else, I will change into something else depending on my next destination or activity. I have a lot of clothes so I choose to wear them even if I am changing several times a day. This is how I get to enjoy more of my clothing and life at the same time. If you like to take selfies or pose for social media often, this can also be helpful for your aesthetic.

How to Win in Life

Be who you want to be. Do not allow anyone to tell you how to live your best life unless they are contributing to it and allowing you to be the director. You are a unique individual and will always be you. You are winning in life if you love who you are when you wake up each morning, and before you go to bed at night. I love who I am and I love who I have grown into and I love me in every stage of my level up. This is the way you win in life. Never base your life on the approval of others. As long as you approve of your life, you win! Your life is your life and you are who you are.

My life is my life and I am who I AM. You are always going to be a creator and you are always going to have the power to create the life you want through your thinking, what you choose to do and how you decide to live each day. I love the life I have created and I love to help other people realize that they can do the same and win in life.

There is no use of seeking approval from others who don't even approve of themselves. So love who you are and love your experiences in this life and focus on what makes you happy.

What keeps you full of joy and living the most blissfully luxurious comfortable life that you can live? No one else is going to give you the permission that you are seeking to live life on your terms. So start living it today and level up your thinking to know that you will win if you are who you want to be with no apologies. Many say life is a game, but you are the creator of the game of your life. So be creative and love each moment of the powerful gift of being a creator, the main character of your own story.

Live your life like you mean it and help others learn to do the same.

Life can be what you make it if you put in the effort to create it each day. They never teach you this in school, so you have to come to this notion on your own. When you have solved this mystery and start to create your own life each day exactly how you want to live it, then you too will have the bliss and life you have always wanted. Winning is when you feel that you can fully enjoy the life you have created and to appreciate every moment of it.

At no matter what level you are in life, you can always live each day in luxury and comfort. Stay focused on what you want your life to be, and you will live it. Now go and live the life you've created and have fun creating it each day. Stay true to yourself and never allow anyone to make you doubt that you can have the luxury and comfort in life that can be obtained by everyone.

225

If you have not yet read my book titled, "How To Do What You Love" available on Amazon, this is a great book on how to start a small business with little to nothing, getting started and how to grow your interests and hobbies to generate an income.

I would like to also say thank you to everyone who chose to read this book and have started creating the life that you have always wanted.

Those who find it harder to level up, I hope this book was helpful to you and that you find your best self and love who you are.

To all my YouTube subscribers: I also want to say thank you from the bottom of my heart.

Without you, I would not be the woman I have grown into thus far. Ya'll keep me laughing and loving what I do each day!

Create Your Life.
Love,

Printed in France by Amazon
Brétigny-sur-Orge, FR